T0277142

Cambridge Elements ☰

Elements in Global Development Studies
edited by
Peter Ho
Zhejiang University
Servaas Storm
Delft University of Technology

THE PROBLEM OF PRIVATE HEALTH INSURANCE

Insights from Middle-Income Countries

Susan F Murray
King's College London

CAMBRIDGE
UNIVERSITY PRESS

Shaftesbury Road, Cambridge CB2 8EA, United Kingdom

One Liberty Plaza, 20th Floor, New York, NY 10006, USA

477 Williamstown Road, Port Melbourne, VIC 3207, Australia

314–321, 3rd Floor, Plot 3, Splendor Forum, Jasola District Centre,
New Delhi – 110025, India

103 Penang Road, #05–06/07, Visioncrest Commercial, Singapore 238467

Cambridge University Press is part of Cambridge University Press & Assessment,
a department of the University of Cambridge.

We share the University's mission to contribute to society through the pursuit of
education, learning and research at the highest international levels of excellence.

www.cambridge.org
Information on this title: www.cambridge.org/9781009507561

DOI: 10.1017/9781009208178

First published 2024

A catalogue record for this publication is available from the British Library.

ISBN 978-1-009-50756-1 Hardback
ISBN 978-1-009-20818-5 Paperback
ISSN 2634-0313 (online)
ISSN 2634-0305 (print)

The Problem of Private Health Insurance

Insights from Middle-Income Countries

Elements in Global Development Studies

DOI: 10.1017/9781009208178
First published online: March 2024

Susan F Murray
King's College London

Author for correspondence: Susan F Murray, susan_fairley.murray@kcl.ac.uk

Abstract: Financial markets, actors, institutions, and technologies are increasingly determining which kinds of services and 'welfare' are available, how these are narrated, and what comes to represent the 'common sense' in the policy world and in everyday life. This Element problematises the rationale and operation of one such financial technology, private health insurance, and the industry it inhabits. It offers a cross-disciplinary overview of the various drivers of these markets in middle-income countries and their appeal for development institutions and for governments. Using a range of illustrative case examples and drawing on critical scholarship, it considers how new markets are pursued and how states are entangled with market development. It reflects on how the private health insurance sector in turn is shaping and segmenting health systems, and also our ideas about rights, fairness, and responsibility.

This Element also has a video abstract: www.cambridge.org/EGDS_Murray

Keywords: private health insurance, insurance industry, health systems, financialisation, middle-income countries

ISBNs: 9781009507561 (HB), 9781009208185 (PB), 9781009208178 (OC)
ISSNs: 2634-0313 (online), 2634-0305 (print)

Contents

1 Introduction   1

2 Development Goals, Health Policy, and Privatism   9

3 Entangled States   16

4 Corporate Commercial Strategies and Industry Influence   27

5 Questioning the Narrative   29

6 States as Market Regulators   34

7 The Political Economy of the Private Health Insurance Industry   41

8 Contemporary Private Health Insurance Regimes   44

9 Final Observations   60

List of Abbreviations   66

References   68

1 Introduction

Financial markets, actors, institutions, and technologies are increasingly determining which kinds of services and 'welfare' are available, how these are narrated, and what comes to represent the 'common sense' in the policy world and in everyday life. This volume sets out to problematise one such financial technology in middle-income countries: 'private' health insurance and the industry it inhabits.

The context of this inquiry is middle-income countries. These are home to 75 per cent of the world's population, including expanding middle classes and the majority of the world's poor. In economic terms, they represent about one-third of global gross domestic product (GDP) and are major engines of global growth (World Bank 2022b). It is not difficult to see why this group of countries is of great importance to the future of the healthcare industry and related insurance markets. Global per capita spending on health is predicted to increase by 50 per cent over this current decade, and much of this growth will be concentrated in middle-income countries (Deloitte 2019; Dieleman *et al.* 2017).

For its part, health insurance is reported to be the fastest-growing segment of the global insurance industry. It reached a value of US$1,590 billion in 2021, with excited predictions of this market reaching US$3,039 billion in 2028 at a compound annual growth rate of 5.5 per cent (Fortune Business Insights 2022). Prior to the COVID-19 epidemic, the health segment of the insurance industry made up just over one-quarter of global insurance premiums (Binder *et al.* 2021b). The segment had primarily been sustained by its operations in the United States of America, which accounted for around 70 per cent of health premiums in 2015 (Binder & Mußhoff 2017: 29). But now a shift in momentum to the emerging markets is anticipated as income levels rise, coverage widens, and more private health insurers enter regional markets.

In particular, industry sights are set on the 'underpenetrated' liberalised market economies and large populations of the Asia Pacific region, which contributed 22 per cent of the €69 billion absolute growth in total health premiums in 2019 (Binder *et al.* 2021a). The COVID-19 pandemic brought a sudden and visible increase in risks to health and life in that region, as it did around the world. It also brought a harsh awareness of the debilitatingly prohibitive costs of treatment in private hospitals. This provided new opportunities to the insurance industry, which was quick to respond. Thai insurers Dhipaya Insurance and Muangthai Insurance launched COVID-19 microinsurance products, and Dhipaya claimed it sold half a million such policies in the first quarter of 2020 (Chung *et al.* 2020). In China, health insurance became the fastest-growing insurance category in the industry. In 2020, low-premium high-deductible 'Huiminbao' supplementary medical insurance was rolled out, led by the local government and underwritten by insurance companies in over 158 cities in 21 provinces, with over 20 million people paying more than an aggregate 1 billion yuan (US$150 million) in premiums (Shanghai Municipal People's Government 2020). By the following year, 140 million people had bought such policies (Leng 2022).

In India, the commercial health insurance sector was still small, but it was gaining traction and business was brisk there too. Only 6 per cent of the population had supplementary plans before the start of the epidemic (Thomson *et al.* 2020b: 26), but then the uptake of private health insurance plans from April to September 2020 overtook that of car insurance, the previous industry leader (Srinivas 2020). Max Bupa Health Insurance, for example, reported a 16 per cent growth in new business in May of that year alone and was confidently expecting that trend to continue (Chakrabarty 2020). When claims increased sharply in the second wave of the pandemic, the Insurance Regulatory and Development Authority of India (IRDA) came to the rescue, allowing a 5 per cent revision in premium rates to help out the insurers (Laskar 2022). Star Health, India's largest stand-alone health insurance company, was among those reporting losses, but it was still able to use the long-term growth prospects to seek new investment and attempt to be listed on the local stock exchange (ET Bureau 2021). By the end of the same year, CareEdge, the Indian analytics and credit rating agency, proclaimed health insurance to be 'a bright spot amidst the pandemic blues', and forecast continued growth at a 16–18 per cent compound annual growth rate for the period 2023–8 (CareEdge 2021).

It seems indisputable that the business opportunities abound. But what does this mean for people's access to good and timely healthcare? How and why has private health insurance become accepted and integrated into health systems in the contemporary period? And what are the implications for social relations?

1.1 Concepts, Methods, and Sources

This volume aims to offer a multidimensional critique of private health insurance. To do this, it draws on a range of literatures and perspectives from the economic and social sciences. Private insurance practice and its regulation in middle-income countries are the subjects of a growing body of health economics, public administration, and policy literature (e.g. Drechsler & Jütting 2005a, 2005b, 2007; Ettelt & Roman-Urrestarazu 2020; McIntyre & McLeod 2020; McLeod & McIntyre 2020; Preker *et al.* 2007, 2010; Sekhri & Savedoff 2005, 2006; Thomas 2016; Thomson *et al.* 2020a; Wu *et al.* 2020). These employ varied degrees of enthusiasm or caution and critique within their disciplinary and technical parameters. The edited volume 'Private Health Insurance: History, Politics and Performance' (Thomson *et al.* 2020a) offers one of the most substantial recent analyses of the impact of private health insurance using multiple comparative high- and middle-income country case studies. The authors consider its influence on health system performance, financial protection, access to health services, and efficiency and quality in health service organisation and delivery. Their findings will be returned to in Section 5.

Critical social policy analysis has also been important in this field. It has informed the analysis in this volume by highlighting a number of interrelated processes taking place within 'health system reform' across the world. These include the sale or transfer of state-owned assets into private hands (privatisation), and also increasingly commercial behaviour by publicly owned bodies. Mackintosh and Koivusalo were among the first to distinguish 'commercialisation' as an important analytical descriptor of what has been taking place in parts of the health sector (Mackintosh & Koivusalo 2005). While the term is sometimes used rather loosely in the literature, their influential framing recognised two aspects: the provision of healthcare services through market relationships to those able to pay, and the investment in, and production of, those services (and of inputs to them) for cash income or profit.

This conceptualisation was taken forward by Tritter *et al.* (2009), writing on European health systems. Here the term commercialisation is used to describe both the engagement of commercial providers in the provision of publicly funded services, as well as the regulatory framework and priorities that shape the provision of services by both public and private providers. Subsequent contributions include Koivusalo and Sexton (2016) writing on gender and commercialisation in healthcare, Murray (2016) on the growth of commercialisation in maternity care, and Baru and Nundy (2020) on China's shift to 'market socialism' and the resultant fragmentation of the health service system.

The related term 'commodification' refers to when activities for health financing and provision are given a monetary value and start being negotiated according to market logic, with different agents buying and selling health goods and services (Cordilha 2022). Scholars in different fields have highlighted that health is being converted from being a right and entitlement to being a privately purchased commodity (Prince 2017). This is accompanied by a redefinition of individuals as healthcare consumers, whose consumption of particular health-related goods and services is shaped not simply by perceived health benefits but also by their associations with particular images, lifestyles, and tastes (Henderson & Petersen 2002; Tritter *et al.* 2009).

An important element of the literature on medical travel highlights its relationship to commodification of healthcare (Ormond 2013) and the role of states and other brokers in developing these markets. For example, Chee (2007) describes the Malaysian state's intimate and direct involvement in the commodification of healthcare by promoting medical tourism via tax incentives, institutional infrastructure for upholding standards and quality, and by leading in the marketing through trade missions and other promotional activities. Connell (2013) similarly argues that contemporary medical tourism is a function of the growing privatisation and commodification of healthcare, where the ability to pay has become the key to obtaining medical care. It is for this reason that Lunt *et al.* (2011) favour the term 'medical tourism' rather than its alternatives, arguing that it draws due attention to the commodification and commercialisation of health travel. Writing on marketisation as the entangling of state and markets, Birch and Siemiatycki highlight that private financing and monetisation of public goods necessarily entails, on the one hand, the commodification of public services, their provision, and their delivery, and, on the other hand, the regulation of these commodification practices by bringing them within the purview of 'the state as market-maker' (Birch & Siemiatycki 2016: 193).

This volume builds on, and extends, this existing literature on commercialisation, commodification, and marketisation, offering a critical analysis of the phenomenon of private health insurance and its market growth in middle-income countries. Drawing on multidisciplinary viewpoints and empirical examples, it examines a range of interrelated dimensions, including the influences of global governance, constitutional rights, states as market makers, and industry interests and actions. It considers the impact on health, implications for social stratification, and the influence on societal relations and behaviours. In doing so, it argues that the influence of private health insurance extends far beyond its percentage contribution to health spending. There are important implications across the health system in terms of the allocation of resources and inequity of access. Across society, private insurance reinforces individualism and social distinctions and increasingly acts as a mode of governance of behaviour.

The overview brings together available evidence, existing experience, and conceptual thinking. The analysis relies upon a close reading of research and policy documents on health systems and their financing, as well as knowledge acquired through two decades of research on health systems in middle-income countries. Sources include a literature review, coverage in the business press media, and primary data from qualitative interviews conducted in Chile, India, and China during a series of interrelated studies on the privatisation, commercialisation, and financialisation of healthcare.[1] These are employed to explore the expansion and operation of this industry in middle-income countries covering case examples from Chile, Brazil, and Colombia – as early adopters, and contemporary developments in emerging economies such as India, South Africa, Türkiye, and China. For the analysis presented in Section 8.1, digital business and popular press media coverage were obtained through Google Alerts over a twelve-month period. This material serves as a source of data in order to scrutinise the discursive construction of the contemporary health insurance market in India.

The intention is not to provide comparative case studies of health system performance in a series of countries, a type of analysis ably done by others (see Thomson *et al.* 2020a). Rather, examples from different countries are employed to illustrate the themes and issues that a probing examination of private health insurance raises. Put another way, the focus is to problematise private health insurance using real-world experiences and to elaborate further on practical and theoretical understanding. The trajectories in five countries (Chile, Brazil, China, India, and South Africa) are presented in some detail, and two others (Colombia and Türkiye) are referred to more briefly. Between them, these countries include several of the world's largest markets for the health insurance industry – existing and potential, countries in which private health insurance is an established element of health system financing, and those where the industry is opening up new frontiers.

Table 1 offers a snapshot of the seven countries. This indicates population size; a recent World Bank estimate of their progress toward universal health coverage (UHC) (a concept discussed further in Section 2); the spending on health in each prior to the COVID-19 epidemic, as collated in the System of Health Accounts;[2] and estimates of the percentage of the population in each

---

[1] Social and structural factors influencing high caesarean section rates in Chile. (1995–7). Overseas Development Agency Health and Population Division (UK): RD352.
Healthcare under Chilean neoliberalisation: Places, spaces and practices. (2015–16). Santiago.
Practices, regulation and accountability in the evolving private healthcare sector: Lessons from Maharashtra State, India. (2017–19). Co-I: I. Chakravarthi. Medical Research Council (Joint Funded Initiatives): MR/R003009/1.
Deconstructing the financialisation of healthcare. Co-I: B. Hunter.
Analysing the transnational provisioning of services in the social sector: The case of commercialisation of NHS services in China and India. (2019–22). Co-Is: R. Bisht, B. Hunter, B. Salter, Y. Zhou. Economic and Social Research Council: ES/S010920/1.

[2] An internationally agreed systematisation of information on financial flows related to healthcare in different countries.

Table 1 Characteristics of coverage and spending on health in Brazil, Chile, China, Colombia, India, South Africa, and Türkiye.

Country and population size (2021 rounded) [a]	World Bank Country income classification [b]	UCH achievement (%) [c]	Spending on health (2019 or nearest available year) [d]				Percentage of pop. with private (commercial) health insurance cover
			Public spending on health as a share of GDP (%)	Govt/compulsory schemes' spending on health as a share of current spending on health (%)	Voluntary private health insurance as a share of current spending on health (%)	Out-of-pocket payments as a share of current spending on health (%)	
Brazil – 214 million	Upper-middle	74.9	3.9	40.9	31.1	24.9	26 [e]
Chile – 19 million	High income[3]	83.1	5.7	60.6	6.6	32.8	>46 [f]
China – 1.4 billion	Upper-middle	71.1	3.0	56.1	8.7	35.2	4 [g]
Colombia – 51 million	Upper-middle	73.0	6.3	77.4	8.4	14.1	49 [h]
India – 1.4 billion	Lower-middle	57.4	1	33.1	11.6	54.8	6 [e]
South Africa – 60 million	Upper-middle	78.5	4.4	48.2	46.1	5.7	16 [e]
Türkiye – 85 million	Upper-middle	55.5	3.4	77.7	5.3	17.0	7.6 [i]

Sources: [a]World Bank (2022b); [b] World Bank (2022a); [c] World Bank (2020): this analysis by Wagstaff & Neelsen (2020) uses an index that captures both health service coverage and financial protection from high out-of-pocket medical spending; [d] Organisation for Economic Co-operation and Development (2022a); [e] Thomson et al. (2020b: 26); [f] Organisation for Economic Co-operation and Development (2022b): while 17 per cent have healthcare cover from health plans with ISAPREs and 46 per cent have complementary health insurance policies, it is not possible to determine the overlap between these groups; [g] Chen et al. (2022); [h] Ministerio de Salud y Protección Social (2022): this percentage represents the section of Colombia's population with mandatory membership of the 'contributory regime' run by private insurers; [i] Organisation for Economic Co-operation and Development & European Union (2018: 175).

---

[3] Chile moved up into the high-income classification in 2006 but was considered to be middle-income during the period described in Section 3.1 when its substitutive private insurance policy was introduced.

country with commercial health insurance cover. The presentation of this data is intended to be descriptive and to give a sense of range among the cases, rather than to offer a ranking within any category or to suggest there are simple causal relationships between the data in different columns. It should be noted that reliable estimates of the percentage of a population with private insurance cover are hard to come by and represent differing points in time, types of sources, and definition.

The data in Table 1 indicate that there are wide variations in the proportion of public spending on health, and also in the extent that so-called 'voluntary' private health insurance currently contributes to spending on health. Thomson and colleagues' analysis of global spending data shows that in 2017, voluntary private health insurance accounted for more than 10 per cent of current spending on health in only twenty-three countries, half of these being middle-income (Thomson *et al.* 2020b: 21). On average, at that time, voluntary private health insurance accounted for an average of 2.4 per cent in lower middle-income countries and 6.3 per cent in upper middle-income countries, but there was a great deal of variation at the country level, particularly in upper middle-income countries.

Does the data on the proportion of current spending on health mean that private health insurance is just not that significant? There are three rather different points that need to be made here. Firstly, the current extensive market-making activity suggests that the role of private insurance within spending on health will be changing in the future for some countries, especially those with expanding middle classes. Indeed, the 'big growth stories' for the insurance industry are forecast to be India and China, due to their economic growth and large population sizes,[4] and their respective governments' embrace of market economy approaches in the sphere of health (Binder *et al.* 2021b; Preker *et al.* 2010).

Second, the percentage contribution to health spending may be a useful indicator, but it provides a limited picture. As some of the illustrative cases in this volume will demonstrate, there are other impacts that private health insurance can have on health systems, especially over the longer term. Private health insurance is key to sustaining and expanding for-profit hospitals and diagnostics sectors, with implications for resource allocation. Furthermore, it redefines the way access to healthcare is thought about.

Third, we need to interrogate the term 'private health insurance'. How does its definition set the parameters for what questions are asked? What does it

---

[4] India represents 17.85 per cent and China represents 17.81 per cent of the world population (World Population Review 2023).

reveal, and what does it hide? In the health financing literature, private health insurance is often defined as 'insurance that is taken up voluntarily and paid for privately, either by individuals or by employers on behalf of employees' (Thomson *et al.* 2020b: 3). It is treated as a technical category, but it is more than this. The emphasis on voluntary serves to reinforce the neoliberal notion that private health insurance is about the creation of choice. The emphasis on voluntary also means that compulsory health insurance managed by private health insurance companies in Chile is not categorised as private health insurance in the internationally standardised definitions for spending in health. Instead, this sits under 'government/compulsory pre-payment schemes' (column 5 of Table 1). The same applies to Colombia's mandatory health insurance, where the funds collected by the government flow on to feed managed competition between forty-five private insurers (Garcia-Ramirez & Nikoloski 2021). This obscures the actual breadth and embedded nature of the insurance industry activity within some health systems. The definitional focus on 'take up', the demand side, also de-emphasises that the insurance is economic activity conducted with the intention to make a profit, before going on to fund for-profit healthcare companies. Private health insurance is the accepted term, and for that reason it is used in this volume, but 'commercial health insurance' would be a more accurate descriptor, as indicated in the final column of Table 1.

This volume will draw on multidisciplinary perspectives to consider private health insurance and examine it from different angles. It is divided into eight main sections, starting with issues of policy and market development. Section 2 describes how and why the global policy environment has favoured health insurance industry growth in the contemporary period, and it considers the experiences of early adopters, including those now trying to disentangle themselves from its legacies. Sections 3 and 4 explore state and industry strategies in several of the world's largest potential markets. Sections 5 and 6 summarise key critiques of the effectiveness of private health insurance that have been articulated within health policy and systems debates and bring together some of the experiences of state attempts at regulating the sector. The final sections widen the analytical lens. Section 7 highlights the changing nature of the industry and its role within transnational financial services and the political economy. Then, building on contributions from sociology and social anthropology, Section 8 articulates the extent of its broader influence over institutions and everyday life through the concept of *a private health insurance regime*. This is illustrated through examples from South Africa and India exploring private health insurance's relationship to class, social differentiation, consumption, and individualism.

It also draws attention to the largely unseen role that it plays in the regulation of behaviour through technologies of surveillance and notions of consumer rights in access to healthcare.

2 Development Goals, Health Policy, and Privatism

In order to understand the place and future of private health insurance within health policy in middle-income countries, it is important to consider the way healthcare financing has come to be understood in the contemporary context. There are four main sources of funding for healthcare services that are commonly cited in the economics and health policy literature. These are general taxation, social insurance, private insurance, and direct payments by users, sometimes referred to as out-of-pocket payments. To what extent health services in a country are protected from commodification will depend, in part, upon the way the system articulates healthcare finance to access to health services (Yilmaz 2013).

Significantly, in recent policy and public discourse, private health insurance has achieved a high profile. It has been portrayed variously as the answer to overstretched public healthcare systems, as a transitional step to publicly provided UHC (Sekhri & Savedoff 2005), as the sensible response for a head of household to the risks of catastrophic private healthcare costs, and as the embodiment of 'freedom' and the right to choice. We need to examine the social and political influences that have led to this in specific countries, and to this end, the cases of Chile, Brazil, and China will be considered in Section 3. But first, this section offers a reflection on the recent history of the internationally agreed goal of UHC and how international agencies have helped to open up the markets for the health insurance industry in the majority world.

The transnational transmission and mediation of ideas and processes, as well as their spread through epistemic communities, have been important in this policy diffusion (Tritter *et al.* 2009). The Millennium Development Goals of 2000, followed by the UN Sustainable Development Goals (SDGs) of 2016, succeeded in focusing the attention of international organisations and national governments on health as a necessary contributor to development. But they did more than this. It was through the circulating concept of UHC and the call for low- and middle-income countries to 'invest in health' that health insurance became globalised. The result was, as Birn and colleagues argue in their blistering analysis of the history of UHC, 'the most remarkable contemporary co-optation of the global health equity agenda' (Birn *et al.* 2016: 745). The terminology itself was telling. As Birn and Nervi point out, more recent use of the term 'coverage' stems from the early twentieth-century US insurance industry, referring to the amount of protection given by a policy. 'However, coverage of what, for whom, how, and so on has remained vague' (Birn & Nervi 2019: 2).

The SDGs committed governments to achieve UHC by 2030, with a focus on measurable 'essential' (not comprehensive) services and on financial protection. The way UHC (not provision) was promoted involved the creation of health insurance schemes which allow people to access healthcare facilities run by public, private, and not-for-profit sectors (Lethbridge 2017). While the resulting insurance arrangements ostensibly increased UHC, they often involved premiums, coinsurance, co-payments, and prohibitive deductibles that impeded actual access.

This was an era of 'privatism': the promotion of the role of the private sector in the provisioning and regulation of all aspects of social and economic life (Slater & Tonkiss 2000). What was happening in health occurred within a broader scenario of active attempts by state and non-state actors to create new markets and opportunities for capital accumulation in the name of 'development' (Hunter and Murray 2019; Mawdsley *et al*. 2018). Now, growing roles for private sources of finance were justified as a strategy to fill the estimated annual gap of US$2.5 trillion required to achieve the SDGs globally, a gap considered beyond the capability of public financing (World Bank and International Monetary Fund 2015).

US$371 billion annually has been estimated as necessary to achieve targets for SDG 3 alone, the goal to 'ensure healthy lives and promote wellbeing' (Stenberg *et al*. 2017). Private investment in healthcare provision and financing became presented as the only solution for addressing geographic gaps in healthcare provision, high mortality, and catastrophic out-of-pocket expenditures.

A supporting role for private health insurance was then needed in order to provide stable revenue streams to private sector healthcare providers. The approach was articulated in the World Bank's advocacy for a global marketplace for private health insurance to complement a new 'multi-pillar approach to healthcare financing in low- and middle-income countries' (Preker *et al*. 2010: 25). Health insurance and for-pay care were accepted as a desirable and common-sense solution to health needs 'in addition to a public health insurance scheme' (Almasi *et al*. 2018).

This soon came to be promoted as a suitable technical fix for countries with a weak tax base and high out-of-pocket payments for healthcare. It was claimed that extending private health insurance would replace out-of-pocket payments for private healthcare, promote solidarity, and 'enable risk sharing' and that governments should adapt their healthcare financing models to facilitate this. However, this ignored the reality that it is 'actuarial fairness' – the equal treatment for equal risks – that underpins commercial insurance models, not social solidarity or subsidy. Furthermore, a key characteristic of insurance in the neoliberal era has been increasing risk segmentation, that is to say, the un-pooling of risk (Ericson *et al.* 2000b).

In some parts of the world, the groundwork for all of this had been laid much earlier. In the 1990s, the World Bank had exercised its more heavyweight loan and grant-giving power to replace the World Health Organization (WHO) as the lead agency in global health policy (Abbasi 1999). It published *Investing in Health* as its 1993 World Development Report (World Bank 1993). This has been described by a notable critic as 'the seminal report of the Bank's transfer of neo-liberal policy measures to the health sectors of the developing world' (Lee 2009: 112). As Dao (2018) found in her case study of Vietnam, in practice 'investment in health' often translated into the further retreat of the state in the health system as the government shifted funding to become a payer and regulator rather than a provider of healthcare.

In Latin America, such shifts had already been engineered in many cases very comprehensively. The redesign and commodification of Chile's health system was a domestic reform of the public sector provision strongly influenced by the US economist Milton Friedman. This was instigated in the 1980s as part of the shrinkage of the welfare state under the military regime of Pinochet and required salaried workers to opt to either pay into the National Health Fund or into new private insurance schemes. The overstretched and underfunded National Health Fund also covered the unsalaried. Because basic 'coverage' could be achieved on key healthcare indicators, Chile has often been held up as a model for other low and middle-income countries to follow. But the reality, as further discussed in Section 3, was a substitutive, socially segmented, and deeply inequitable system, described by Thomson *et al.* (2020b) as the most egregious of the seventeen private health insurance systems in wealthy and middle-income country systems that they analysed.

Other countries on the continent did not fare much better (see also the account by Birn *et al.* 2016). In the period 1993–9, healthcare reforms took place in at least thirteen Latin American and Caribbean countries, supported by World Bank and Inter-American Development Bank loans, often as part of a larger package of reforms including pension schemes. The activities financed by the loans included the design of new healthcare systems, strengthening the agencies responsible for designing and regulating health policy, providing healthcare for low-income groups, decentralising health services, and conducting research on health policy. As an analysis by Armada *et al.* (2001) has shown, regardless of the type of intervention, most of these initiatives favoured the private financing and provision of healthcare over the public financing and provision that had predominated previously.

This move from public to 'private solutions' represented a major shift in the financing, delivery, and ownership of health services. For example, the Colombian 1993 reform of its healthcare system, guided by the World Bank and the International Monetary Fund, and implemented through Law 100, introduced a mandatory health insurance model based on managed competition between private insurers. It comprised four elements (Alvarez *et al.* 2011). The first of these was a split of purchasing and providing functions, and effectively a privatisation of the care delivery system so that the public hospitals and health centres in urban and rural zones became private institutions. They were no longer to be directed by the public health planning function of the health ministry or receive funds from the state at national or municipal level. The second, individual health insurance was to be the mechanism for receiving healthcare, with two branches, a contributive system, and a subsidised system, run by private health insurance companies. Third, a basic benefit was to be developed, including medical procedures, hospitalisations, and medicines that insurance companies must guarantee to their enrolees; anything not included in the plans would require private purchase. Fourth, the public health programmes were to be commodified into a series of individual programmes, such as vaccinations or health education sessions, which health insurance companies could provide individually to their members.

Three decades after this was rolled out, health service researchers began to highlight the problems that ensued. The 'managed competition' resulted in various different contracting arrangements and models of care, plus fragmentation in the continuum of care. On top of this, pre-authorisation requirements were being employed to limit the use of services, and denial of services was not infrequent (Vargas et al. 2010). There were lengthy legal battles between citizens and insurance companies (Abadía-Barrero 2016).

The World Bank has staff from more than one epistemic community, although there is little question that economist viewpoints and the finance agenda dominate. Deacon (2007) indicates that there were disputes between the public health professionals, who were then organised in the Population Health and Nutrition Division, and the health economists in the policy unit and operational teams. While Richard Feachem was Director for Health, Nutrition and Population, his new sector strategy emphasized equity as well as efficiency. The strategy document stated that 'insurance plans ... often exclude those who need health insurance the most' (World Bank 1997: 5 quoted in Deacon 2007: 57). It concluded that 'private health insurance is not a viable option for risk pooling at the national level in low or middle income countries' (World Bank 1997: 8), and it advocated for strong, direct government intervention to finance public health activities.

That position was crowded out. Currently, the World Bank views the relatively small fraction that voluntary private health insurance represents in current health expenditure in developing countries as a problem to be solved. It sees 'one of the most critical health-financing questions' to be 'whether it is possible to mobilize voluntary direct contributions to prepaid and pooled funding from people working in the informal economy'. This is couched within a mission 'to overcome impediments to financial inclusion' (World Bank 2019: 52).

The Bank's report on High-Performance Health Financing for Universal Health Coverage (2019) suggests several ingenious ways to 'generate step-changes in health-financing policy'. These include mobile-based insurance products that take automated deductions from unrelated financial flows, for example, mobile phone payments or remittances, and the bundling of insurance with other products and services that offer immediate benefits to consumers. The focus on making people available, through their health needs, to businesses (Ellison 2014) could not be clearer: 'flows of funds that these innovations could tap point to potentially outstanding returns on investment, for example, the roughly half trillion dollars of out-of-pocket payments or the approximately half trillion dollars of remittance flows to developing countries' (World Bank 2019: 52).

Among the UN agencies, the International Labour Organization was notable for standing its ground in arguing for social health insurance as opposed to private health insurance, although it accepted that some publicly mandated health insurance might be implemented by private insurance companies (see Tessier *et al.* 2020). For its part, the WHO struggled to maintain a clear counter-position, and during her appointment as its Director General, Gro Brundtland sought to improve the economics-based evidence of the WHO's work and to use this evidence to set priorities (Lee 2009). The organisation's autonomy was severely compromised by its 2000 World Health Report on health systems, which appeared to abandon the Health For All strategy and the goal of providing health services according to need, and to accept a transition to market-oriented practices and increased individual responsibility. Its approach shifted attention to contractual arrangements for organising healthcare systems and for privileging an emphasis on cost effectiveness over one on social inequalities and equity of access (Braveman *et al.* 2001; Ollila & Koivusalo 2002).

Critics within and outside the organisation highlighted that many of the central authors of the WHO report were former or present employees of the World Bank or had played a crucial role in the production of its *Investing in Health* document. They also noted that in the meeting of health system experts who dealt with the report at its drafting stage, representatives from the health ministries of the member states were heavily outnumbered by other participants who represented the World Bank, the Organisation for Economic Co-operation and Development (OECD), universities, private health services, and health insurance institutions (Ollila & Koivusalo 2002). This shift in representation away from consultation with WHO's own constituency was a manifestation of the growing influence of SDG 17, which argues for the role of multi-stakeholder partnerships including commercial actors,[5] for achieving the other SDGs.

Internally to WHO, contestation continued. The WHO's substantial draft report, 'Public Health and Trade: A Guide to the Multilateral Trade Agreement', gave a stark warning that 'unless prevented by law, regulation or contract, private health insurance companies in order to be more profitable will drop high-cost patients, refuse coverage for those with pre-existing conditions and diseases, and limit benefits'. Similarly, 'for-profit hospitals will not provide free care to the poor unless required by law to provide a minimum amount' (quoted in Deacon 2007: 87). However, the tenor of the final report, which was published jointly with the World Trade Organization, was far less cautionary.

The WHO fully endorsed UHC in 2010, but the Pan American Health Organization continued to refer to 'comprehensive health services' in its strategy documents and took up the term 'universal health' to overcome the dilemmas over 'coverage' (Birn & Nervi 2019). Latterly, the debates led by WHO have largely been about the issue of risk pooling[6] and its implementation within the context of UHC. For example, senior staff in the Department of Health Systems Governance and Financing at WHO have consistently focused on raising the profile of pooling as a health financing policy instrument, providing analyses of country pooling arrangements and the challenges typically associated with how fragmentation manifests in each setting (Kutzin *et al.* 2016; Mathauer *et al.* 2019; Sparkes *et al.* 2019). The WHO's position on voluntary health insurance is that it 'needs to be managed and regulated in such a way that it contributes to equitable progress towards UHC, or at least does not harm such progress' (Mathauer & Kutzin 2018: 7).

Beyond the World Bank, other members of the World Bank Group were clear on their priorities. The International Finance Corporation (IFC), for example, complements the work of the World Bank in public sector reform by focusing on the development of the private sector (Lethbridge 2005b). It exists to promote the flow of private sector capital to developing countries and acts as a channel

---

[5] Several scholars since have studied the expansion of public–private partnerships (PPPs) generated around the world by SDG17. Among others, Miraftab (2004) argues that the PPPs are a 'Trojan horse' in development, enabling the insertion of markets in the provision of public goods.

[6] Risk pooling is a means to redistribute from lower-need to higher-need individuals by de-linking contributions such as taxes or insurance premiums from their health risk. A single pool would maximise the potential for risk pooling across the whole population.

for venture capital to encourage industrial development (Deacon 2007). In 2001, the IFC established its own Health and Education Department to encourage such investments in these sectors and to loan funds for such purposes (Lethbridge 2005b).

The IFC began to promote private sector investment in a range of aspects of health service provision in countries in South and East Asia, Africa, the Middle East, and Latin America and parts of Europe. This included loans to holding companies that directly encourage new forms of private delivery or to health insurance companies; for example, a loan of US$22 million was made to ORESA Ventures, which then created the Medicover (Central and Eastern Europe) health insurance company (Lethbridge 2005b).

The World Trade Organization is not commonly thought of as an international agency that determines health policy. However, the binding policies and obligations arising from trade and investment agreements can affect how governments regulate and organise health systems (Koivusalo *et al.* 2021). Economic globalisation has played a key role in the spread of private health insurance, the growing scale of cross-border trade of commodities and services, the flow of international capital, and the wide and rapid spread of technologies (Shangquan 2000).

The overarching aim of the World Trade Organization General Agreement on Trade in Services (GATS) is to encourage countries to open up their service sectors to foreign competition. Once a country has agreed to sign up for GATS for a specific service, it must treat firms from all nations equally in terms of market access. Many see this as a back-door route to increasing the private market share of hitherto publicly provided services (Deacon 2007). But while governments tend to be cautious about signing up for trade agreements on health services, insurance is covered under the financial-service and insurance-service sector in GATS. Insurance services, like other financial services, have frequently been included in schedules of specific commitments (Adlung 2010).

In 2022, the World Bank and the World Trade Organization offered a post-COVID-19 action plan that governments could implement to strengthen trade's contribution to future global health security. *Trade Therapy: Deepening Cooperation to Strengthen Pandemic Defenses* was premised on the argument that trade in medical goods and services had been an essential weapon in the battle against the coronavirus (COVID-19) pandemic. It also suggested that further trade liberalisation would assist cooperation in future pandemics.

Despite acknowledging research showing that 'the overall effect of private health insurance on UHC is ambiguous', the report went on to claim that 'appropriately regulated' private health insurance played an important role in the 'health care global value chain' (World Bank & World Trade Organization 2022: 24). Foreign health insurance suppliers were also said to be positively contributing to the uptake of private health insurance by bringing capital, technology, and know-how. Recommendations included easing the portability of health insurance coverage and reducing foreign investment barriers as ways to help widen the health insurance market and thus contribute to expanding health insurance coverage.

3 Entangled States

Health system financing is a subject of interest for influential global policy-makers, but ultimately, it is produced in places. The market opportunities for the global insurance industry are determined not only by global forces but also by local conditions. And the political history of private health insurance takes place in parliaments, legal courts, regulatory agencies, and in the lobbying and media influencing by the insurance industry associations (Ossandón 2015).

In Europe, private health insurance largely began before publicly funded insurance, centred around employment and loss of income from illness. This was mirrored in South Africa, where private schemes were introduced at the turn of the twentieth century, under British rule, for white mine workers (McIntyre & McLeod 2020). In other middle-income countries, private health insurance emerged following government decisions to enhance private involvement in the health system after some form of national health insurance had already been established (Thomson *et al.* 2020b).

This section considers some specific examples of situations where states have actively encouraged the growth of the health insurance industry. Firstly, it explores the trajectories of two early implementers: Chile and Brazil, both with relatively large proportions of the population with some sort of private health insurance cover (over 46 per cent and 26 per cent respectively). One of the reasons these provide an interesting, if sobering, comparison is because they have contrasting constitutionally enshrined rights to health. Their experiences over time raise important questions about the notions of freedom of choice and of 'complementary' healthcare systems that often underpin the official justifications for private health insurance.

These are followed by the case of the more recent market development in China. This large country has moved in two decades from a complete state monopoly of health insurance to an official view that the Chinese government should actively develop commercial health insurance, and a situation where an estimated 30 per cent of the urban population held private health insurance policies. In China, private health insurance is largely provided by comprehensive insurance firms which also provide policies for life insurance, property insurance, and car insurance (Shi & Lui 2018). This case thus gives insight into the state as maker of broader insurance markets.

The final part sets out some other areas of state-market entanglement where new opportunities are offered to the industry by middle-income countries' decisions to develop sites for medical tourism and by social insurance programmes that require their management expertise.

3.1 Creating Freedom of Choice? The Case of Chile

When former student activist Gabriel Boric was elected to the Presidency of the Republic of Chile at the end of 2021, he did so on a platform of social demands. Among these were a commitment to a single Universal Health System and an end to the segregated system of Instituciones de Salud Previsional (ISAPREs), the private enterprises that ran the country's commercial healthcare insurance plans.

Four decades previously, the ISAPRE system had been introduced to enact the rights set out in Article 19 of the Constitution, which was established during the military rule of Pinochet.[7] The ideological commitment underpinning the Chilean Constitution was to economic liberties, and this Article states that 'each person has the right to choose the health system they wish to join, either public or private'. In practice, as observed by a prominent Chilean legal scholar, it was a constitution 'according freedom of choice only to those who could afford it' (Soloman 2014).

As Rose argues in his seminal analysis of political power, freedom is not the opposite of government but one of its key inventions and most significant resources (Rose 1999). The Chilean state now became an active market-maker for the 'freedom' of private health insurance. Commentators have observed that Chile's (public and private) substitutive[8] model for health insurance coverage is not dissimilar to the one later outlined by the Affordable Care Act in the USA (Vargas Bustamante & Méndez 2016).

Private for-profit firms, ISAPREs, were permitted to compete for the administration of health contributions. These contributions were defined as a part of

---

[7] The Boric government's attempt to adopt a new progressive constitution was defeated overwhelmingly in a plebiscite in September 2022 after a storm of disinformation about what it would signify. See Bartlett (2022a; 2022b).

[8] Supplementary private health insurance is a way of obtaining prepaid access to private facilities, avoiding waiting times for publicly financed specialist treatment or benefiting from enhanced amenities in public facilities. Complementary private health insurance fills gaps that occur when the publicly financed benefits package is not comprehensive in scope or involves user co-payments. Substitutive private health insurance occurs when people are allowed to choose between placing their funds in public and private coverage. See Thomson *et al.* (2000b: 3).

the salary of each worker (originally 4 per cent, today 7 per cent of the salary), compulsorily withdrawn every month to finance medical expenses (Ossandón & Ureta 2019). Employer-provided health insurance was eliminated, and shopping for health insurance coverage became the sole responsibility of individual consumers. As with the privatised pension system created at the same time, workers were understood as investors who could choose where to place their monthly contribution, whether with the National Health Fund (Fondo Nacional de Salud) or with one of the ISAPREs (Ossandón & Ureta 2019).

Within ten years, the ISAPREs had become a profitable industry, administering contributions from more than 1.5 million users (out of a total population of 15 million), most of whom were from the wealthier sectors of the population (Ossandón & Ureta 2019). They were also directly or indirectly connected to a growing network of private healthcare infrastructure. For example, Banmédica was originally a company that provided healthcare to bank clerks but had become a large corporation by the end of the 1990s. Its network of companies includes an ISAPRE, life insurance, emergency paramedic care, and a real estate business. It has also moved into the international arena with joint ventures in pension funds in Peru (AFP Horizonte) and Argentina (AFJP Previar), and with a healthcare provider in Colombia (Salud Colmena). In 1997, after acquiring another healthcare provider and a hospital, Banmédica reported income of over $260 million and coverage of 800,000 people in its Chilean healthcare business (Armada *et al.* 2001).

The private health plans on offer were openly discriminatory. While the amount paid every month to the National Health Fund was simply 7 per cent of the users' salary, ISAPREs were allowed to risk-price on the basis of sex and age. Until 2010, the ISAPREs used risk charts that discriminated against older people and against women. Women of reproductive age were regularly sold plans with no or very low obstetric or neonatal cover, referred to as 'planes sin útero' (literally 'plans without uterus'). This effectively excluded reimbursement for the hospital care that they were most likely to use (Gideon & Alvarez Minte 2016).

Once these health plans were finally banned on the grounds of gender discrimination in 2019, the prices for health plans for women in this age group rose immediately by an average of 3.4 per cent (Chekh 2020). There was no cross-subsidy from male subscribers; the average price of a plan for a man in that age group reduced by 2.3 per cent at the same time. Chile's example may seem at the extreme end of the spectrum, but as Doyle has pointed out, medical underwriting, target marketing, and un-pooling in search of smaller, less risky pools is a common insurance industry practice. Further afield, it was only in March 2011 that the European Court of Justice took the decision to prohibit differential risk rating on the basis of gender (Doyle 2011).

Chile's population became segmented into two groups: the higher-income low-risk individuals who were profitable for private health plans, and people who were unable to afford private coverage or were excluded from it. For a long time, ISAPREs were allowed to deny coverage for 'pre-existing' medical events, such as chronic or serious past diseases that users had before contracting their policy (Cid *et al.* 2013). In reality, a person suffering from a serious chronic disease could not decide to look for a new insurer and had little 'freedom to choose'. The National Health Fund enrolees were the less affluent, sicker, and older individuals. It became a regular practice for ISAPRE enrolees to switch to the National Health Fund when they could no longer afford their private plans in old age. By the mid-2000s, the National Health Fund was insuring approximately 90 per cent of all individuals over sixty-five years of age (Vargas Bustamante & Méndez 2016).

Chile may appear to perform well on basic indicators for 'universal health coverage' but the resources available to each segment are very different. The National Health Fund insures five times as many individuals as the private health insurance system. Yet, it spends half as much on its most costly enrolees as ISAPREs spend on their average enrolees (Vargas Bustamante & Méndez 2016). Most Chilean doctors work in the private healthcare sector and provide care to the small proportion of the population who are privately insured, for greater financial incentives. Now only 44 per cent of physicians have contracts with public providers (Crispi *et al.* 2020). Public hospitals are congested with long waiting times for some investigations and treatment, and their specialist staff either provide insourced private services at weekends to reduce the waiting lists[9] or decamp to work in the private facilities. Latterly, the National Health Fund has had to buy services for its own enrolees from these private hospitals.[10]

Private health insurance has also transformed clinical practice in some areas, as private facilities and doctors honed their practice to fit the reimbursement policies set out in the plans. For example, in the more expensive private health plans that did include pregnancy cover, reimbursement was for labour care and delivery conducted by a private obstetrician. Delivery by a midwife was not reimbursable, even though professional midwives attend the vaginal births in Chile's public sector.[11] Many of these private obstetricians had limited availability to be on-call. So, this scenario, combined with families' desire to avoid incurring the higher co-payment charges for care during the night and at

---

[9] Source: Interview with director of public hospital, Santiago 2015. Healthcare under Chilean neoliberalisation: places, spaces and practices project.

[10] For example, the prevalence of births in private facilities covered by public insurance increased from just 1.6 per cent in 2001 to 20.6 per cent in 2014 (Borrescio-Higa & Valdés 2019).

[11] Source: Social and structural factors influencing high caesarean section rates in Chile project

weekends, escalated rates of intervention. This resulted in extraordinarily high caesarean section rates in privately insured patients (Murray & Elston 2005).

It is very clear that, over time, Chile's 'freedom to choose' health insurance set-up shaped a two-tier healthcare system that fostered the growth of a large private healthcare provision sector, while depriving the public sector of finance and specialist human resources. In doing so, it replicated structural inequalities of class in access to healthcare and in highly differential quality of provision. The fragmented risk pools and segmentation of service quality became normalised and entrenched in the assumptions of everyday lives, epitomised by the explanation proffered by a hospital project manager that 'healthcare is much like a carcass of beef. Not everyone can have the prime cuts'.[12]

3.2 A Complementary Private Sector? The Case of Brazil

Brazil has a very different constitutional statement about the health rights of its citizens, but its trajectory shows how powerful industry opposition can undermine this. After the Brazilian military regime ended in 1985, Brazil underwent a process of healthcare reform that culminated in the recognition of healthcare as a right of citizenship and the creation of the public, universal Unified Health System (Sistema Único de Saúde, SUS) enshrined in the Constitution of 1988:

> Health is a right to be enjoyed by all and a duty of the State; it shall be guaranteed by economic and social policies that aim to reduce the risk of disease and other maladies and by universal and equal access to all activities and services for its promotion, protection, and recovery.

This system was intended to be tax-funded, comprehensive, and universally accessible to all Brazilians, free of charge, regardless of their economic or social status. Brazil was the only country on the continent to propose a universalistic health reform in the 1980s, in striking contrast to the predominant neoliberal trends in healthcare reform elsewhere in Latin America (Machado & Silva 2019).

However, Brazil already had an important private health sector with private hospitals contracted by public social security institutions, as well as a growing sector of private health insurance plans. These groups pressured legislators to avoid proposals that could result in a radical shift toward state control and the imposition of constraints on the private sector (Machado & Silva 2019). So, while the 1988 Constitution recognised health as a universal right that the state was required to provide, it also affirmed the private sector as complementary, with priority for philanthropic and non-profit institutions. Furthermore, it stated

---

that healthcare would be 'open for private investment', thus retaining openings for expansion of the private system. It was this last clause that set the ground for the future.

By 2013, the Brazilian healthcare market was being promoted as 'one of the most promising and attractive in the world' by PwC, a global Big Four accounting firm (PwC 2013). Brazil's private health insurance market had grown to become the world's second largest following the USA, with an overall turnover for the private health insurance sector of R$145 billion in 2018 (Scheffer *et al.* 2020). There were now some 1,226 health insurance and plans companies. The largest of these were Assistência Médica, controlled by US-based UnitedHealth with 3.52 million 'beneficiaries' and Bradesco Saúde, a subsidiary of Bradesco Seguros, the health insurance arm of local banking giant Bradesco covering 3.26 million (Bnamericas 2019).

Private health insurance gives access to care in private hospitals for about a quarter of the Brazilian population, mainly better-off households living in urban areas in the south-east covered by group plans through their employers (Montoya Diaz *et al.* 2020: 66). However, their vulnerability in this arrangement was illustrated when Brazil experienced a severe economic crisis from mid-2014 onwards. Some 2.6 million people had their private health insurance cancelled either because they lost their jobs and benefits or they could no longer afford the premium (Greca & Fitzgerald 2019). They then had to turn to the increasingly overstretched SUS for their care.

Unlike the Chilean system, private health insurance in Brazil is voluntary and supplementary to the SUS. However, the Brazilian state, too, has been an active market-maker for the industry. It supports the private insurance industry with tax subsidies. Individuals and legal entities can deduct health costs, including private health insurance, from their taxable expenses. Studies by Ocké-Reis and others have found that these concessions expanded both the private health insurance market and the supply of private hospitals (Ocké-Reis 1995 cited in Montoya Diaz *et al.* 2020).

Indeed, despite the constitutional declaration that was in defiance of the regional trend, subsequent successive Brazilian governments have rolled back their commitment to a single unified public system and consolidated the commercial sector. One administration after another raised the cap that limited tax deductions on private healthcare spending, and it was eliminated altogether in 2005 under President Lula and the Workers' Party government (Lavinas 2017). Emblematically, in 2006, Brazil's civil servants became doubly incentivised to shift to the private sector: as individual income tax payers they were already entitled to the deductions, but also the state would now return part of the cost of their premium to them by via their payroll.

A constitution is often understood to be a body of fundamental principles. However, it is, only as effective as the policymakers wish it to be. In 2016, Brazil's newly appointed Health Minister under President Temer, Ricardo Barros, gave a newspaper interview about the constitutional definition of access to healthcare as a universal right. His reply was brisk and dismissive:

> We aren't going to be able to maintain the level of rights guaranteed by the Constitution. At some point, we're going to have to reassess things, like the Greeks did when they cut pensions, as well as other countries that reassessed the obligations of the state because they no longer had the capacity to sustain them ... The more people that have insurance, the better, because it means they pay for their own care, which eases the financial pressure on the government. (Collucci 2016)

This attitude toward the limits of state obligations continued with the fiscal policies of the recent Bolsonaro government. Brazil's public healthcare system was hit badly by the president's denialism and chaotic response to the COVID-19 pandemic. Almost 700,000 people died of COVID-19 in Brazil, one of the highest death rates worldwide, and screening, diagnosis, and treatment of other diseases, including cancers, were severely affected. Yet the SUS budget set for 2023 by Bolsonaro's outgoing government represented a substantial cut of almost R$23 billion (around £3.6 billion), reducing the budget to the lowest level in ten years (Triufol 2022). Meanwhile, in response to the private health industry's complaints about rising costs, the National Supplementary Health Agency announced a 15.5 per cent hike in health insurance premiums, the biggest in twenty-two years, for all individual and family healthcare plans[13] (Marshall 2022).

3.3 A Market in the Making: The Case of China

Governments are often complicit with the health insurance industry for the reasons that Minister Barros cited in Brazil. But beyond this, state involvement in the broader insurance market formation and development is also widespread (Ericson *et al.* 2000b). Markets for commercial health insurance in middle-income countries have often evolved as part of broader attempts to encourage an expansion and stability of the insurance industry or of financial services as a whole,[14] or as a result of trade agreements.

---

[13] Collective corporate plans were excluded from the adjustment, presumably to protect employers from increased costs.

[14] Insurance laws, for example, can affect the activities that are pursued. It has been noted in the context of Europe and Solvency II that if strict solvency requirements are imposed on the insurance industry, this can incentivise for-profit insurance companies to diversify, notably on more secured markets such as healthcare (Benoît *et al.* 2021).

China provides an example of recent state-led insurance market development in one of the world's most populous countries and the evolution of commercial health insurance within it. The previously state-owned monopoly was dissolved in 1988 when Ping An Insurance Company, a shareholder-owned insurer, was allowed to enter the insurance market. Then, in 1992, the People's Bank of China granted American International Group, Inc. (AIG) a license to sell individual life insurance, marking the opening of the Chinese insurance market to foreign firms. The American International Underwriters, one of AIG's affiliates, set up the first foreign Property and Casualty branch in Shanghai three years later. Between 1992 and 1998, ten joint ventures and foreign branches obtained licenses to write insurance in China. In order to protect the nascent Chinese domestic industry, China's regulatory policy was based on a 'gradual, paced' approach to permitting foreign competitors into the insurance market (Leverty *et al.* 2009).

The development of private health insurance as a supplement to China's primarily public health insurance was featured in the 9th Five-Year Plan in 1996. The World Bank had been working with the Ministry of Health and then its replacement, the National Health and Family Planning Commission, in a series of projects related to health system reform. 'Analytical and Advisory Activities' undertaken under the auspices of its China Rural Health project included a review of healthcare financing and an assessment of healthcare delivery systems in China (Hu & Ying 2010; World Bank 2004).

It seemed that China was joining the global epistemic community. Later, in 2016, the World Bank Group released the report 'Healthy China' with recommendations for healthcare reforms in China based on a health sector study that was undertaken jointly with the WHO and three Ministries of the Chinese Government. Under the overall leadership of the Chinese Finance Minister and the WBG Managing Director, the study was financed by the International Bank for Reconstruction and Development (IBRD), with contributions from the IFC and the Bill and Melinda Gates Foundation via the Results for Development Trust Fund. This was followed by a US $600 million IBRD health sector reform Program-for-Results to transform health service delivery for over 100 million residents in Anhui and Fujian provinces and to provide lessons for China and beyond (World Bank 2018).

Even more importantly for the global insurance industry, China had joined the World Trade Organization in 2001 (Zhang & Yang 2007). This opened up the domestic insurance market to international funders. Among other things, it resulted in commitments to enhance the scope for foreign life insurers by allowing them to set up health insurance businesses in a joint venture format. Elimination of geographical restrictions also meant that if they operated for three years in China, they could then expand their provision of health insurance to most Chinese cities rather than being limited to certain big cities like Beijing and Shanghai (Sun 2005: 85). On the domestic side, PICC Health, China's first commercial health insurance company, was established in 2005.

Liberalisation continued: in 2006, the central bank permitted qualified insurers to purchase foreign exchange for investment in products with fixed returns abroad. The same year, it was announced that Chinese insurers would be allowed to invest in the listed and unlisted equities of domestic banks, strengthening cooperation among the country's insurance, banking, and securities sectors. Commercial banks were also allowed to set up insurance businesses (China Daily 2006). In 2007, the China Insurance Regulatory Commission raised the limit for overseas investment by Chinese insurance companies from 5 to 15 per cent of their assets. In 2008, China's State Council gave approval for insurers to buy equity in private (non-listed) firms in an effort to widen their investment channels (Chiang 2008).

During their period in government, President Hu Jintao and Wen Jiabao, Premier of the State Council, both indicated the importance of the health insurance industry. In 2011, McKinsey research reported that by then approximately 30 per cent of China's urban population possessed some kind of private health insurance, while another approximately 20 per cent 'was planning to buy' some form of health insurance in the near future. Much of this was an 'add-on' purchased as part of a product bundle or as a rider on savings products or life and accident insurance products (Ng *et al.* 2012: 77). All of the top ten life insurers and seven of the top ten property insurers in China were now offering private health insurance (Chen & Lin 2012).

Vice Premier Li Keqiang, an economist by profession, sparked fresh interest in 2012 when he wrote in the official Party newspaper that the Chinese government should 'actively develop commercial health insurance' and 'facilitate the integration of basic medical insurance and commercial medical insurance'. Two years later, the State Council, China's cabinet, issued 'Opinions on Speeding Up Development of Commercial Health Insurance' an administrative document to encourage private insurance in the healthcare sector (Shi & Liu 2018). The following year, a trial programme of pre-tax reductions for commercial health insurance premium payments of less than 2,400 yuan (US$392) was launched with the aim of making the burgeoning Chinese private hospital sector more financially viable and thereby reducing pressure on government services (Lei 2015).

From then on, commercial health insurance grew rapidly, outpacing other types of insurance. From 2014 to 2018, the compound annual growth rate of China's commercial health insurance was 36 per cent, 17 per cent for life insurance, and 11 per cent for Property and Casualty insurance (Yi & Huang 2019). After consolidating the domestic industry, in April 2018, China announced the gradual lifting of restrictions on foreign insurers, allowing companies that were 100 per cent foreign-owned to operate in the country. Within seven months, Allianz received permission to set up a wholly owned insurance holding company in Shanghai. Soon after, AXA agreed to acquire the remaining 50 per cent stake it did not already own in AXA Tianping Property & Casualty Insurance.

As of 2018, commercial health insurance premiums accounted for 14 per cent of the total insurance premium income in China (Yi & Huang 2019). Total premium revenue for commercial health insurance products grew from US$33.7 billion (RMB 241.1 billion) in 2015 to US$98.9 billion (RMB 706.6 billion) in 2019. Currently, about 95 per cent of China's population receives some form of public health insurance after a huge reform of the public insurance system, but it is domestic 'insurance giants' like Ping An and China Life that offer commercial products which cover critical illness, medical reimbursement, disability income, and long-term care.

3.4 Other State-Created Opportunities for Industry Expansion

Middle-income countries have become hosts to wider private healthcare and hospital markets for the cosmetic surgery industry and healthcare tourism. India and Thailand's introduction of expedited medical visas, for example, is a sign of their commitment to facilitating trade in medical tourism (Johnston *et al.* 2010). While governments of middle-income countries are 'reimagining healthcare as an industry, alert to the potential to profit from goods ... and a spectrum of care services' healthcare has become less enshrined as a public good and increasingly framed as a commodity via international trade agreements (Ormond 2013: 5).

This has manifested in the emergence of a new market in specialist travel insurance for medical tourists (Lunt *et al.* 2011). Insurance products for high-end users have emerged in the global marketplace that provide coverage for medical procedures, travel companions, medical complications, trip cancellation and interruption, evacuation, and repatriation. There was a period when USA insurers put a toe in the water too. Aetna paired with an HMO in Mexico, and Blue Cross Blue Shield piloted insurance in several states, enabling patients to have expensive surgical procedures at low-cost offshore medical facilities. But it was premature to claim, as some did, that the insurance industry in the USA had become an active participant in medical tourism (Horowitz *et al.* 2007). Interest fell away after the Affordable Care Act changed the financial incentive for US citizens to undertake cross-border medical travel by capping out-of-pocket costs for high-deductible health plans (Lendner 2018).

It may seem counter-intuitive, but state health insurance schemes can also provide opportunities for industry expansion. This is because, through UHC, insurance corporations gain access to public revenue streams such as social security contributions and taxes that finance contracts to provide a set of services to the previously uninsured (Birn *et al.* 2016). Commercial insurers are brought in to guide on data analysis and advise on the design of payment reform, as well as to manage programmes.

In China, the governments of Fujian province and Chongqing were early adopters in contracting private insurance companies to manage public schemes, drawing on private companies' expertise in areas like benefit design, enrolment, and provider management. In return, private insurance companies had opportunities to extend brand influence and cross-sell life insurance products to consumers. Local governments also organised collaborations between hospitals and private insurers, paving the way for the development of a local private health insurance market. The most common collaboration was in 'instant claim initiatives', in which bills are settled before the patient is discharged. The cities of Wuxi and Tianjin and the provinces of Henan, Shaanxi, Shanxi, and Hunan all ran pilot programmes in this area (Chen & Lin 2012).

The Indian federal government increasingly finances healthcare for the poor through subsidised private health insurance. Firstly, it introduced the Universal Health Insurance (UHI) scheme, also referred to as the 'Government Rupee-a-Day' scheme. Termed a 'public–private partnership' in line with the discourse of SDG 17, this attempted to extend private health insurance to those living below the poverty level through central government premium subsidies. In 2007, after the lack of success in uptake of UHI, the Indian government launched Rashtriya Swasthya Bima Yojana (RSBY), literally 'National Health Insurance', a scheme for people living below the poverty line that provides annual hospitalisation coverage up to Rs 30,000 for a family of five and some coverage for transportation, with no exemption of pre-existing diseases (Montoya Diaz *et al.* 2020). In 2016, RSBY covered over 41 million people (around 3 per cent of the population).[15]

As with its predecessor, RSBY was government-funded but relied heavily on private health insurance operators to carry it out. Each state government selected the implementing insurance company (public or private) through

---

[15] The RSBY programme initially came under the Ministry of Labour and Employment. It was shifted to the Ministry of Health and Family Welfare and renamed as Rashtriya Swasthya Suraksha Yojana (RSSY), and later was renamed again as National Health Protection Scheme in the 2017–18 budget.

a tendering process. In addition to their normal role of providing insurance, the contracted operators had to manage the scheme from start to finish. They were required to enrol a predefined list of households below the poverty level, contract nongovernmental organisations to conduct information and awareness campaigns, set up a kiosk in each village to manage the scheme, provide a toll-free call centre, contract both public and private government-accredited hospitals, and deliver direct reimbursement of providers (Jain 2010).

This deepening cooperation between insurers and government agencies on social insurance in the health sector not only provides the industry with new lines of revenue but also means that the public systems are ever closer in design and form to the commercial systems, sharing much of their logic and assumptions.

4 Corporate Commercial Strategies and Industry Influence

Other interested actors in the private health insurance markets in middle-income countries include private healthcare companies, which aim to meet the demands of an expanding middle class for hospital-based and technologically advanced healthcare. Such companies advocate for a division of activity between governments serving those on low incomes and providing 'basic' care, and their own role in providing for the better-off. The development of this strategy is dependent on the creation of a market for private insurance and its integration with private provision[16] (Lethbridge 2005a).

In Chile, financing from the health plans run by the ISAPREs supported the expansion of the 'clinicas', private sector hospitals offering accommodation that ranges from relatively modest to luxurious. Between 2011 and 2020 the number of beds in private clinics increased by over 16 per cent, while the nation-wide increase was only 0.8 per cent (Clínicas de Chile 2022: 21). In Asian countries, health insurance similarly plays an important and expanding role in enabling middle-class groups to access private healthcare. Viewing the expansion of private health insurance and private health services as complementary market processes, a regional healthcare company based in Singapore was one of the first to start its own managed care programme. In 2000 Parkway launched a joint venture with Allianz, a large European insurance company, to combine insurance and provision of care

---

[16] In some high-income countries with extensive public systems, like the UK, contracting to the public sector is a larger market for them than the provision of private insurance. This can take various forms. For example, 'provider collaboratives': Groups of public and private providers such as Cygnet, Priory and Elysium that will be responsible for designing services for NHS England (Pollock & Roderick 2021), and insourcing, where a private business carries out work on the public hospital premises (see NHS Shared Business Services 2018) . As mentioned, similar practices have been growing in Chile.

(Lethbridge 2015). Five years later, Parkway had 40,000 members in Singapore and was looking to expand their programme to Malaysia and Indonesia, targeting high end patients (Lethbridge 2005a: 27).

Lethbridge's research indicates that company strategy is strongly influenced by both the historical background of the companies and the current market context in the healthcare arena. Conversely, multinational companies are skilful players in influencing national markets and political environments in their own interests (Lethbridge 2005a, 2011). Corporations use political practices to secure a favourable policy environment. These political practices include argument-based discursive strategies and action-based instrumental strategies.

Discursive strategies, for example, may include stressing the crucial role the corporation plays in the economy through jobs and investments, and their essential contribution in sustaining healthcare provision (Mialon 2020). In Chile this argument has been used on several occasions by private health insurance companies. It was employed in 2016 after ISAPREs subscribers had filed more than 130,000 injunctions against the raising of their premiums. Judges not only ruled in the complainants' favour in all these cases but also obliged the insurers to pay the legal fees. Immediately, the spectre of the health insurance companies being 'pushed to the brink of collapse' and the predicted consequent implosion of the private healthcare sector was invoked, along with a threat that the holding companies might have to 'look elsewhere' and no longer invest in activities in Chile (Bloomberg 2016). The threat of impending bankruptcy was used again in 2022 when the Supreme Court accepted appeals filed against six of the private health insurance companies and ordered them to suspend the 'arbitrary' annual increases of 7.6 per cent applied to premiums of their basic health plans (Cooperativa.cl 2022).

The insurance industry also employs common action-based instrumental strategies. These include preference shaping and information management, the building of alliances with third parties such as doctors' organisations or with the press media (illustrated in Section 8.1), and direct involvement and influence in policy. This last is done through lobbying, provision of financial incentives to politicians, and participation in working groups and technical meetings with governments. For example, in order to formulate an 'accessible health insurance project' for low-income families in Brazil, the Ministry of Health brought together a working group that included the Brazilian Insurance Federation.[17] This ensured that the highly restricted plans met the commercial needs of the industry (Bahia *et al.* 2016a).

---

[17] The National Confederation of General Insurance, Private Pensions and Life, and Supplementary Health and Capitalization (CNSeg) brings together key actors of the insurance

The insurance industry can capture elected officials who vote for the interests of their elite funders (McKee & Stuckler 2018). Brazil provides an example of how extensively this can operate. In the elections of 2010, health insurance companies allocated R$11.8 million in official donations to the campaigns of 153 candidates for elective office. This contributed to the election of thirty-eight federal deputies, twenty-six state legislators, five senators, five governors, and the president. Eighty-two candidates received support but were not elected (Scheffer & Bahia 2013). Then, for the 2014 elections, insurance companies and executives donated R$54.9 million to electoral campaigns, contributing to the election of three senators and thirty federal representatives, including Ricardo Barros, who was to become the Minister of Health under Temer (Bahia *et al.* 2016a).

Chile, proud of its reputation as relatively corruption-free, was rocked by a probe into a holding company, the Penta Group, in 2015. This group had banking and insurance operations and controlled the private health insurance company Banmédica and its clinical networks mentioned earlier in this section. The owners, some staff, and employees of the Chilean National Tax System were prosecuted for using fake receipts to dodge taxes and then redirecting funds to the political campaigns of the right-wing Independent Democratic Union (UDI) politicians. Several Penta Group employees, and some of their family members, were convicted of tax evasion, bribery, and money laundering. The directors of Penta Bank were penalised with paying a fine, spending a few days in a special prison for economic crimes, and attending mandatory business ethics classes. The leniency of their sentence caused considerable popular outrage. As one of the protest banners read at the time: 'Cárcel para los pobres, clases de ética para los poderosos': 'Prison for the poor, ethics classes for the powerful' (Ruiz 2019).

5 Questioning the Narrative

A 'trade narrative' is an account of how an industry operates, usually developed by a trade association or lobbying group. Such a narrative aims to put a positive light on the benefits of the industry's contribution to the economy or social agenda and to distract from the underlying economic and financial dynamics of the industry (Burns *et al.* 2016). Recently, careful critiques of private health insurance have come from health economists working on health financing and systems. These challenge the trade narrative about who benefits from the industry and the role it plays within health systems. Key among them are Thomson *et al.*'s (2020a) volume for the European Observatory on Health

---

industry, coordinates political actions, elaborates strategic sector planning, and conducts activities in the common interest of the four Federations.

Systems and Policies, which reviews detailed country case studies from high- and middle-income countries to consider the evidence base for a range of commonly heard claims, and the analyses conducted by Kutzin and colleagues of the Department of Governance and Financing at the WHO (see Mathauer & Kutzin 2018).

The first question concerns whether promoting private health insurance is a successful strategy for the reduction of out-of-pocket payments. That relationship was not borne out when Thomson *et al.* (2020b) analysed data from WHO's Global Health Expenditure Database. When they examined the relationship between voluntary private health insurance and the out-of-pocket payment share of current spending on health, they found this to be very weak. Importantly, across countries there was a much stronger association between public spending on health and out-of-pocket payments. In other words, increases in public spending on health are much more likely to reduce gaps in coverage than increases in spending through voluntary private health insurance.

The second question concerns the argument that a private insurance sector for those who can afford it frees up government resources to provide health insurance for low-income individuals. This is a popular notion, but it is also overly simplistic on several counts. The reality is that over time, resources are extracted from the public sector, with major consequences for the quality of care it can provide. In countries where the private insurance sector sustains the private healthcare provision sector, as in South Africa, the rate of doctors per 100,000 people can be more than five times higher in the private sector than in the public sector (McIntyre & McLeod 2020; McLeod & McIntyre 2020).

On top of this, in substitutive systems like that of Chile, the publicly financed coverage loses higher-than-average income-related contributions when people opt for private health insurance. This is because those opting out are more likely to come from richer groups. This loss of contributions from richer people is compounded by the fact that public funds cover a pool with a higher-than-average risk of ill health than the private health insurance pool. Even in substitutive systems, the borders between public and private coverage are porous. Older and sicker people return to the public sector when they can no longer afford the premiums of the private plans.

Another area of porosity occurs when some people covered by private health insurance also continue to use public facilities. In Brazil, this is permitted by law with compensation to be paid by the private insurers to the public facilities. However, in practice, achieving reimbursement is cumbersome and costly. Lavinas has described how between 2000 and 2017, Brazil's National Agency of Supplementary Health (ANS) demanded around R$6.6 billion in compensation. But by 2017, only about 24 per cent had been collected and remitted to the

National Health Fund, with R$2.1 billion (32 per cent of total ANS claims) being pursued through the judicial system (Lavinas 2017: 33).

Furthermore, far from freeing up government resources, tax relief on private health insurance premiums constitutes an indirect form of public subsidy to the commercial sector. All the middle-income countries used in illustration in this volume (Chile, Brazil, China, South Africa, India, Türkiye, and Colombia) have used or trialled such incentives, despite a marked effect on the availability of public funds for healthcare.

Tax subsidies have been shown to be particularly inappropriate in markets for supplementary private health insurance, which are heavily skewed in favour of the richest and healthier sections of the population (Thomson *et al.* 2020b). Brazil and South Africa are notable examples. Tax subsidies for private health insurance amount to around 30 per cent of federal government spending on health in Brazil and around 30 per cent of all government spending on health in South Africa.[18] In Brazil, this is compounded by tax waivers on household spending on private healthcare including cosmetic surgery and other non-essential interventions. So, while private health insurance benefits some people, generally those who are already socially and economically advantaged, it often has negative consequences for the public purse.

A third, related question concerns whether a strategy of expansion of private health insurance will assist countries in achieving UHC targets. Findings published in *The Lancet* by leading researchers from the World Bank's own Development Research Group provide good grounds to question this. The complex analysis of UHC indicators in 111 countries showed that strong performance was correlated with the share of a country's health budget that is channelled through government and social health insurance schemes. On the other hand, associations of UHC with the share of health spending channelled through private insurance were found to be 'ambiguous' (Wagstaff & Neelsen 2020).

A fourth question concerns assertions that private health insurance companies can make strategic purchasing, keep quality up, and prices of private medical treatment down for their clients. Thomson, Sagan, and Mossialos's analysis indicates that, outside of the United States of America, engagement in strategic purchasing[19] has not happened (Thomson *et al.* 2020b). They conclude that very few have been able to exercise leverage over healthcare providers.

---

[18] This is even though private health insurance covers only a fraction of the population, 24 per cent in Brazil and 16 per cent in South Africa (Thomson *et al.* 2020b).

[19] According the 2000 World Health Report, 'Passive purchasing implies following a predetermined budget or simply paying bills when presented. Strategic purchasing involves a continuous search for the best ways to maximise health system performance by deciding which interventions should be purchased, how, and from whom' (World Health Organisation 2000).

India provides one recent example of an insurance company's attempt to exercise that leverage and the struggle between different interest groups, each claiming patient interest and the moral high ground. The issue in this case was the high price of branded medications. In 2017, Prime Minister Modi hinted that a new law was to be brought in to force doctors to prescribe medicines by their generic names. Max Bupa Health Insurance took advantage of the publicity around this and wrote to inform hospitals that they must prescribe medicines only with their generic names for claims to be reimbursed. Compliance was to be with 'immediate' effect. A clear justification for why generic drugs were not used under certain circumstances would have to be written and filed as a part of discharge documentation. Max Bupa Health also warned hospitals that it had the right to retrospectively audit those claims where there are no justifications given for the prescription of more expensive branded drugs. The lobby group of hospital chains in India, the Indian Medical Association Hospital Board of India, fought back by appealing to the notion of professional autonomy, arguing that the insurance company was 'intruding into the right of registered medical practitioners' and that such interference in prescribing 'quality drugs' for patients was 'unwarranted and unethical' (Sinha & Rajagopal 2017).

What has been evidenced is that insurance companies can penetrate private sector hospitals' clinical departments through their daily operational processes and influence the type of activity that is prioritised. But this is not about protecting the interests of subscribers. Generally speaking, medical care has to be documented in ways that can be audited by administrators and by the clinicians employed by insurers and third-party administrators (TPAs) to review claims for reimbursement. As demonstrated by a study in Maharashtra (Hunter *et al.* 2022), the insurance companies establish their own clinical pathways through treatment protocols that set out the tests and treatments to be provided in the event of particular health conditions. These protocols are used to standardise care and enable the capping of fees that will be paid by an insurer, calculated according to a negotiated cost for the package of services. In this way, insurers determine the forms of care that are deemed appropriate to be covered by the insurance, and the items that are considered additional for which patients must settle the bill. This type of strategy is not specific to India. Many insurance companies maintain margins by selecting risks, especially when competing with national health insurance, and by shifting costs onto households through the use of co-payments, benefit ceilings, deductibles, exclusion of high-cost elements such as medications, and medical savings accounts (MSAs) (Thomson et al. 2020b).

Mathauer and Kutzin's (2018) analysis for WHO accumulates the evidence on voluntary health insurance when considered from the technical perspective of progress toward UHC. They reveal a number of what they term 'inherent challenges'. Box 1 presents these in summary as issues directly affecting

Box 1 Summary of the 'inherent challenges' of private health insurance. Adapted from Mathauer and Kutzin (2018).

Issues affecting policyholders	Issues affecting non-policyholders
• High administrative costs of the bureaucracy required to assess risk, rate premiums, design and advertise products, pay commissions, review claims, as well as the duplication of tasks necessitated by fragmented pooling result in higher premiums. • The direct profits made by for-profit insurance companies are taken from the premiums under administration costs. • Premiums are usually risk- or community-rated, thus disconnected to people's ability to pay, and regressive. • Patients get more attention, possibly better quality of care and shorter waiting times, but risk over-provision of diagnostics and health services that are unnecessary and even harmful.	• People with higher health risks and lower incomes cannot afford to purchase a policy and end up using far fewer services/poorer quality services as a result. • Risk selection attempts of insurers to enrol only 'good' risks with expected lower healthcare costs, places the demand for chronic/complex care on public services. • Private health insurance often pays higher remuneration rates to providers, exacerbating inequitable access if patients with coverage get preferential treatment. • Private health insurance finances expansion of private provision with the long-term flight of professionals to work in the private sector and shortages of skilled health workers in government facilities, thus further reinforcing inequities in health service availability. • Financing of private health insurance becomes even more pro-rich when uptake is subsidised through the tax system. • Tax incentives for uptake are an indirect public subsidy that could otherwise supplement to public health budget.

policyholders (practices that result in high administration costs, regressive premiums, and over-intervention) and issues affecting non-policyholders (inequitable access to high-quality services, concentration of chronic and complex care in the public sector, flight of skilled health workers, and tax subsidies that go to the rich rather than the public health budget). Overall, they serve to confirm the highly problematic nature of commercial health insurance practices within a health system.

6 States as Market Regulators

Birch and Siemiatycki's analysis of marketisation emphasises that markets do not replace the state: markets can be instituted by the state and are dependent upon the state for their operation (Birch & Siemiatycki 2016). Governments often have the authority to regulate the insurance business, for example, by setting the reserve requirements. Additionally, private healthcare financing is heavily regulated by governments' tax policy (Cacace & Schmid 2008). Box 2 gives a chronology of key government interventions affecting commercial health insurance markets in five middle-income countries: Brazil, Chile, China, India, and South Africa. This illustrates a largely common trajectory joined by different countries at different time points and an intensification of attempts at regulation interventions by the state as the industry grows in domestic importance and influence.

Market-conduct regulators have been introduced in most countries. These may be specific to the health insurance sector, as in Chile and Brazil, or only cross-industry, as in India. The IRDA, in place in India since 1999, has a dual function to both regulate and develop the insurance market. In terms of regulation, it covers consumer protection through licensing of insurers, regulation of advertising and TPAs,[20] solvency of health insurers through

---

[20] Third-party administrators are firms that emerged in the mid-1990s in India and came under the regulatory remit of the IRDA in 2002, partly to help increase confidence in and uptake of private health insurance. Third-party administrator roles include enrolment of policyholders and dependents into its system, call-centre services including pre-authorisation of hospital expenses, managing access to hospital networks, claims administration including adjudication, processing and settlement of claims, and generating statistics and performance reports. In 2015, TPAs handled over half of all cashless health insurance claims transactions (Montoya Diaz *et al.* 2020). The use of TPAs by insurance companies, as part of their processes for verifying the necessity of treatments provided and negotiating reimbursements with hospitals, aroused criticism from providers over their aggressive renegotiations. It took Public Interest litigation filed in 2011 by an activist, and resulting intervention by Bombay High Court in 2015, to press IDRA into action regarding the behaviour of TPAs. The IDRA then produced guidelines relating to the activities of insurance companies and agents acting on their behalf (Hunter *et al.* 2022). There are currently twenty-three TPAs registered with the IDRA, between them dealing with 181,071 hospitals (Insurance Regulatory and Development Authority of India 2020: 82).

Box 2 Government Interventions in Commercial Health Insurance Markets (Brazil, Chile, China, India, and South Africa). Compiled by the author from sources cited in this volume.

1976	Brazil: Private insurers are allowed to operate.
1981	Chile: Introduction of choice of public or private coverage for the whole population.
1980s to early 1990s	South Africa: Deregulation of the private health insurance market.
1988	Brazil: Constitution declares universal right to health to be delivered through a unified SUS but affirms the complementarity of the private sector.
1994	South Africa: Medical savings accounts established.
1996	China: The development of private health insurance, as a supplement to primarily public health insurance features in the 9th Five-Year Plan.
1998	South Africa: Introduction of material regulation of the private health insurance market with effect from 2000.
1998	Brazil: Congress passes Health Insurance Plan Law.
1999	India: IRDA established to both regulate and develop the insurance market.
2000	Chile: Creation of Superintendencia de ISAPREs as the regulator of private health insurance.
2000	Brazil: Creation of state agency to regulate private health plans.
	All private health insurers in Brazil are mandated to offer a reference plan as an option.
2002	India: Third-party administrators come under the regulation of IRDA.
	Government allows a deduction from taxable pay of premiums up to Rs 15,000 or Rs 20,000 for senior citizens.
2003	Chile: Government requires minimum benefits for private health insurance.
2004	India: National government introduces the 'Rupee-a-Day', UHI scheme, a public–private partnership to extend private health insurance to those living below the poverty level through central government premium subsidies.

(cont.)	
2007	India: IRDA removes tariffs from general insurance, including for private health insurance, with the aim of driving additional growth of the private insurance market. RSBY is launched – a national scheme for people living below the poverty line, government funded but relying on private health insurance companies to administer.
2007	South Africa: Government commits to pursuing a national health insurance system.
2011	South Africa: Green Paper on national health insurance suggests private health insurance could be restricted to 'top-up' insurance (White Paper follows in 2015).
2014	China: State Council issues 'Opinions on Speeding Up Development of Commercial Health Insurance'.
2015	China: State Council launches a trial programme that offers pre-tax reductions for health insurance premium payments of less than 2,400 yuan (US$392) per year.
2015	India: Parliament enacts changes to the Insurance Act of 1938, raising the foreign direct investment (FDI) cap in Indian insurance companies from 26 to 49 per cent.
2017	Brazil: Central government introduces 'accessible private health plans', low-cost, state-subsidised private plans with highly restricted benefits for low-income Brazilians.
2021	India: The foreign investment limit in the insurance sector, including health insurers, was raised from 49 to 74 per cent by the Insurance Amendment Act, 2021, clearing the way for foreign ownership.

minimum capital and surplus laws,[21] regulations and auditing, and oversight of grievance and dispute resolution through an insurance ombudsman system (Montoya Diaz *et al.* 2020).

---

[21] All insurance companies in India are required to maintain a minimum solvency ratio of 150 per cent at all times.

Regulatory systems are often shaped by advisors from other countries with market-oriented systems. For example, contractors supplied by the United States Agency for International Development (USAID) worked extensively with the IRDA and other key stakeholders in India's health insurance sector for a five-year period in the mid-2000s as part of the Indo-US Financial Services Reform and Expansion project (BearingPoint 2008).

6.1 Revolving Doors

The regulators can be focused on the protection of policyholders, on ensuring public confidence in the industry through enhanced transparency, or on prevention of unfair market segmentation practices. But corporations can influence regulatory bodies by placing their advisors on committees or by creating revolving doors where individuals move between employment in public regulators and regulated institutions or take lucrative consultancies (McKee & Stuckler 2018).

In a newspaper interview after retiring from five years as Chair of the IRDA of India in 2013, Hari Narayan is quoted as saying, with remarkable frankness, 'regulators all over the world are very chary over regulating products. And they normally have two reasons to do that. One is that it stifles innovation, and it doesn't allow free market play [but] I think the reasons are much deeper. I think there is a philosophical problem. I think the regulators are probably closer to the industry than they ought to be'. His replacement in the post was T. S. Vijayan, a former Chairman of the Life Insurance Corporation of India (Kaul 2013; Live Mint 2013).

In Brazil, the ANS is the state agency created in 2000 to regulate private health plans. It oversees an industry that was estimated to be worth US$50.2 billion in 2018, for a population of 47.4 million who had private health insurance plans. The ANS has five directors and 1,225 staff with a budget of R$347.2 million (US$88 million) (figures from ANS Annual Report 2018 quoted in Scheffer *et al.*, 2020).

ANS has focused on regulating contracts, systematising information, and organising the market, but never on restricting the growth of the private sector (Machado & Silva 2019). This becomes unsurprising when considered in the light of the close industry-regulatory body links. Scheffer *et al.* (2020) looked at the two main federal health regulatory agencies, the ANS and its sibling National Health Surveillance Agency, which regulates drugs, food, cosmetics, tobacco, and a range of medical products, equipment, and services. They found that almost half of the executives who worked at these agencies had either started in, or ended up working for, private companies that were regulated by these agencies. This is a common pattern in many countries, and it can be compounded when such roles are political appointments and abrupt unemployment occurs with a change in government.

6.2 'Consumer Rights' in Practice

Once established, attempts to diminish the power of insurance companies are often fraught with difficulties. In the 1990s in Chile, the Superintendencia de ISAPREs (later renamed Superintendencia de Salud) was created to regulate all private health insurance plans (Vargas Bustamante & Mendez 2014). This agency, like many others, was directed at what Vargas Bustamante and Mendes call a 'managed consumerist' approach, developing measures to improve the transparency of the private marketplace. This was done by providing information directly to consumers about the performance of the health plans and the insurance companies and was intended to allow them to make more informed choices.

Government regulators also aimed at reducing the number of health plans available in the marketplace through Plan AUGE (Acceso Universal de Garantías Explícitas), which defined the set of specific cost-effective healthcare that all public and private health plans were required to offer. Regulations were also issued on the packaging of additional elective coverage. The number of health plans available in Chile reduced from 40,586 in 1989 to 6,914 in 2005 (Superintendencia de Salud, 2007 figures cited in Vargas Bustamante & Mendez 2016).

However, like many regulatory bodies, the Superintendencia was constrained in the scope of regulations that it could implement beyond this. There was little it could do to minimise exclusionary clauses, pre-existing conditions, and treatment denials (Vargas Bustamante & Méndez 2016). Then, in 2005, all five of the largest commercial health insurers in Chile, which between them controlled about 98 per cent of the market, changed the coverage levels offered to users. Within a year, the health plans referred to as '100/80' that gave 100 per cent coverage for hospitalisations and 80 per cent coverage for ambulatory care were almost fully replaced by plans with only '90/70' coverage. The Superintendencia was aware of this but had no powers to intervene directly.

It fell to Chile's national antitrust prosecutor (Fiscalía Nacional Económica, FNE) to file a lawsuit before the Chilean competition court, the Tribunal de Defensa de la Libre Competencia, accusing the five companies of collusion to reduce the coverage level offered across the sector. It was argued by FNE that the insurers' decision was a coordinated one with the purpose of increasing profits, while the ISAPREs argued that an increase in medical and hospitalisation costs induced them to reduce coverage with the purpose of limiting 'the well-known moral hazard problem' that affects health insurances. The Tribunal, in a split decision (3–2), ruled that there was not enough 'hard' evidence to prove the existence of a collusive agreement (Agostini *et al.* 2008).

State regulators may have the authority to intervene in premium increases and other aspects of the insurance industry, but private insurance premiums are generally set by insurance companies. There have been times when that power has been challenged. Premiums and their coverage may be subject to negotiations if powerful employers are involved. For example, in India's Maharashtra, transnational IT companies secured the inclusion of maternity care coverage in the group plan for their employees' families.[22]

Organised legal recourse in the courts can sometimes be effective. This was demonstrated in 2015 by the rulings in the Chilean courts on 130,000 injunctions against the raising of health plan premiums. In this case, the campaign took on aspects of a social movement, but to take out an injunction requires confidence and knowledge of the legal system, and processes can be lengthy.

Ombudsman systems are sometimes set up to keep claims out of the courts. In India, an ombudsman system was established in 1998 following recognition that the civil courts and consumer protection were ineffective for insurance-related claims because of delays and high expenses (BearingPoint 2008). The Council of Insurance Ombudsmen is composed of eight members: one from the IRDA, one from the Ministry of Finance, plus the MDs and CEOs of six leading insurance companies. The ombudsman is 'required' to pass a decision within three months from the receipt of a complaint, and the awards are supposed to be binding upon insurance companies.

However, the reality has been somewhat different. In 2021, in response to a Right to Information enquiry, it was reported that about 20 per cent of cases in which orders had been issued against insurers for 2019–20 were still outstanding, and in the previous ten years, IRDA had taken no action against any insurer for not complying with orders passed by the insurance ombudsman. In 2018, there was a period in which not one of the seventeen regional offices had an insurance ombudsman in post, and about 6,000–7,000 complaints were reported to have piled up. On average, the ombudsman posts at these offices had been vacant for two to three years (Asia Insurance Review 2018).

The Council of Insurance Ombudsmen's annual report in November 2021 reported that the vacant positions had been filled. Additionally, the report stated that the seventeen offices in the country had received 26,297 complaints during the year, besides 8,722 grievances that were carried forward from 2019–20. COVID-19 related disputes accounted for 39 per cent of the

---

[22] Source: 'Practices, regulation and accountability in the evolving private healthcare sector: Lessons from Maharashtra State, India, project.

total, with nearly 10,000 complaints. Stories in the Indian press demonstrated that many policyholders were bearing the brunt of the disputes between hospitals and insurance companies over COVID-19 treatment costs, including who should pay for the use of vital personal protective equipment (Kulkarni 2020, 2021). Remarkably, many of the so-called 'comprehensive' commercial health insurance plans did not cover 'consumables'. Consumables, which constitute around 20 per cent of COVID-19 hospitalisation bills, are medical aid items that are discarded after single use and include essentials such as syringes, masks, gloves, and personal protective equipment kits.

Only a minority of those with a complaint will go to the ombudsman. Undoubtedly, the use of courts and ombudsman services requires social and cultural capital. Bähre (2016) has described how, in South Africa, predominantly white and relatively wealthy insurance clients could mobilise ombudsman organisations, financial journalists, or legal institutions to express their concerns. But the new, poorer customers were, by and large, unable to use these routes to bring their experiences to attention. Their experiences with misselling, or the refusal to honour legitimate claims or concerns about illegal financial deductions, did not enter the public domain and remained largely out of sight of policymakers and sector regulators.

6.3 Government Attempts at Roll Back

For their part, insurance companies exert their political and financial muscle when their interests are threatened. Governments do sometimes attempt to roll back commercial health insurance and develop National Health Insurance with single funds and single payers. Chile is on the verge of trying to do this under Boric, having failed to do so under Bachelet's presidency despite the majority report recommendations of the Advisory Commission of the Presidency in 2015. South Africa has been moving toward this for about a decade. When attempts to constrain industry expansion are initiated by governments, they tend to be met with vociferous opposition that evokes notions of freedom and rights.

As mentioned, Chile's private health insurance companies proclaimed themselves to be 'on the verge of bankruptcy' after the Boric government indicated its commitment to a single health fund and intention to move their role from substitutive insurance to a complementary model. When the South African government moved to restrict the sale of private 'catastrophic insurance' plans and strengthen the centralised National Health Insurance, industry advocates mounted a campaign of outrage on the grounds of unacceptable restrictions on an individual's 'freedom to choose their own healthcare'.

There was a similar uproar when the South African government made the decision to phase out the primary healthcare insurance policies provided by insurance firms. The Council for Medical Schemes had determined that these private primary care policies were expensive, provided low-value benefits, and over-promised and under-delivered. However, constitutionality, citizens' rights to pursue business, and the rights of poor people to high-quality care were all evoked in a press release from the opposition party, the Democratic Alliance:

> The publication of the 'Demarcation Regulations' by the Minister of Health, Aaron Motsoaledi, and the Minister of Finance, Pravin Gordhan, finally gives effect to the deeply misguided decision to phase out private health insurance for low-income households. This poorly conceived decision demonstrates just how ideologically constrained the Ministers have become when it comes to ensuring that poor South Africans have access to quality healthcare across the country. . . . . This is high-handed, peremptory and likely unconstitutional, for it inhibits the right of every citizen to choose and practice their trade freely. (Wilmot 2017)

The press release went on to suggest that the likely reason for the government action was that it was clearing the way for 'its own state health monopoly', a striking neoliberal term for a National Health Insurance system.

In sum, while commercial health insurance has been widely promoted as part of the solution in the universal healthcare coverage scenario, important evidence suggests that even within its own terms, the trade narrative does not stand up to scrutiny, and that state regulation, while considered 'necessary', is often severely limited or compromised.

7 The Political Economy of the Private Health Insurance Industry

Health insurance companies have had different trajectories in different settings. In China, the health insurance business started from life insurance companies, which had existing clients, the actuarial expertise to set premiums, and could provide capital or a reinsurance fund for health insurance operations (Hu & Ying 2010). Newer actors included pharma and device companies interested in rolling out targeted insurance companies as a means to make their patented products affordable (Ng *et al.* 2012). In countries such as Brazil, they began as smaller companies often dissociated from other financial institutions, or originally developed in the non-profit segment where benefits within the membership group could be based on solidarity principles (Cordilha 2022).

However, there are some striking similarities in the contemporary phase in which we see fewer and bigger insurance companies, with a greater share occupied by the for-profit segment. They often belong to larger financial institutions that are not specialised in health. That broader insurance industry has also undergone fundamental restructuring. This restructuring was driven by economic globalisation, technological changes including digitisation, the integration of the traditional four pillars of financial services (banks, trust companies, insurance companies, and securities dealing), and in particular, the entry of banks into the insurance business and attendant competition resulting in an acceleration in mergers and acquisitions (Ericson *et al.* 2000a). Contemporary private health insurers are increasingly run by finance experts who oversee buyouts and prioritise mergers and speculation (Mulligan 2016). They list on the stock exchange and have a managerial focus on shareholder value.

The trajectory of Inversiones La Construcción (ILC) is illustrative. The ISAPRE Consalud was set up to provide private health insurance for the construction industry in Chile, and ILC was founded in 1980 to manage this and a group of other financial entities in Chile 'that provide key services for the country's development', according to the ILC website. Those other entities include AFP Habitat (pensions), Confuturo (life insurance), Banco Internacional (banking), Red Salud (healthcare provider), and Vida Cámara (supplemental health insurance). Inversiones La Construcción was listed in 2012, raising US$468 million, one of the largest initial public offerings in Chile's history (ILC 2022). With more than 14,500 employees, it includes operations in Chile, Peru, and Colombia. In early 2022, ILC hired two banks, Bank of America and JPMorgan, to lead the sale of up to $400 million in 10-year bonds to pay off debt and add to working capital (Goicochea 2022).

According to the US-based International Trade Administration's country commercial guide, healthcare is a 'best prospect industry sector' for Chile, and US companies have invested heavily in the Chilean healthcare sector over the last seven years, in private provision, pharmacy chains, and insurance: for example, in 2017, Nexus acquired Masvida, one of Chile's twelve ISAPREs. The following year, United Health Group acquired the large private health insurance and medical provider Banmédica, giving the company a presence in Chile, Peru, and Colombia (International Trade Administration, no date).

It is important to emphasise that, as well as being seekers of investment, insurance companies are considerable contributors of investment capital in the political economy. They make most of their profit from investment activity, with little regard for consequences beyond making money from money (Ericson *et al.* 2000b; Mulligan 2016). For example, Mohan *et al.* (2010: 1029) have pointed out the irony that major insurers in the global life and health insurance industry own US$1.88 billion of stock in the five leading fast-food companies, representing 2.2 per cent of the total market capitalisation of these companies.

The insurance industry can act as an important source of long-term funding for businesses and national governments, using a range of financial investment instruments such as government bonds, stocks, and debentures. In the UK, for example, the insurance industry manages investments of £1.8 trillion, which is equivalent to around 25 per cent of the UK's total net worth (Association of British Insurers 2022). China's insurance industry, which is at a much earlier stage of development, reported a roughly similar amount in aggregate assets of CNY18.3 trillion (US$2.73 trillion) at the end of 2018, with a rise of 9.5 per cent compared to twelve months previously (Asia Insurance Review 2019). In January 2022, the aggregate assets stood at CNY25.3 trillion (CEIC 2022), approximately US$3.99 trillion.

Governments often seek to manage the direction of these significant investments and regulate investment practices. India's Investment (Amendment) Regulations of 2001 are an example of guidelines issued by its regulatory authority that aim to control the degree of investments by insurers. In the case of China, a circular on 'Ten Suggestions on the Reform and Development of the Insurance Industry' was issued by the China State Council in 2006. Insurers were encouraged to invest in the capital market directly or indirectly with the investment proportion increased step by step, to invest in more types of securities products, to invest in real estate and venture capital on a trial basis, and to purchase shares in commercial banks. This circular was the first official document of China's central government relating to the insurance industry for twenty years and marked a step change in its commitment to the industry.

Two years later, China's cabinet gave approval for insurers to buy equity in private firms (non-listed companies) in an effort to widen their investment channels (Xinhua News Agency 2007). Then, in 2019, The China Banking and Insurance Regulatory Commission said it would allow insurers to buy Tier 2 capital bonds and perpetual bonds[23] issued by qualified commercial lenders. The regulator aimed in this way to further boost bank capital to curb financial risk and increase lenders' capacity to extend loans (Sio 2019).

As insurance companies become transnational corporates, or come under transnational holding companies, they become more versatile in how they are able to pursue their financial interests, including their ability to circumvent national taxation requirements. Techniques, including 'thin capitalisation', have

---

[23] Tier 1 capital is the primary funding source of the bank and consists of shareholders' equity and retained earnings. Whereas Tier 2 capital includes revaluation reserves, hybrid capital instruments and subordinated term debt, general loan-loss reserves, and undisclosed reserves. It is considered less reliable than Tier 1 capital because it is more difficult to accurately calculate and more difficult to liquidate. The key feature of a perpetual bond is that there is no maturity date. For an investor, it often offers a higher yield than other forms of debt on the market.

been reported in which subsidiaries are developed in countries with lower taxation or where loans between different corporate entities within the same group are used to artificially reduce a company's tax burden. Pursuing such cases requires expertise and resources that may not be available in many middle-income countries.

A recent case prosecuted in Australia was revealing (Marriage 2018). It was related to alleged thin capitalisation practices there by a well-known international health insurance and health and social care group, which is active in many middle-income countries including China, Egypt, Mexico, Bolivia, Brazil, and India. The case is perhaps particularly interesting because the organisation describes itself favourably as a private company without shareholders that reinvests its profits in its services, yet the alleged financial practices were no different from those of for-profit corporates. The subsequent settlement involved no admission of guilt but a payment of a total of \$157 million to the Australian Tax Office, covering penalties and the tax for 2007–18 (Financial Review 2019).

Recent scholarship from economic anthropology and political economy (Bahia *et al.* 2016a, 2016b; Cordilha 2022; Karwowski 2019; Lavinas 2017; Mulligan 2016) suggests that the expansion of the health insurance industry can best be understood as part of the financialisation of social infrastructure. Financial logics, instruments, markets and accumulation strategies, they argue, are having an increasing influence over public institutions. While commodification has continued, the driving underlying process has become 'assetisation', in the sense of assigning properties of a financial asset to something previously not treated as such.

Such assetisation can be seen when activities for health financing and provision are assessed based on risks and returns and transformed into investment opportunities, representing a claim on ownership or contractual rights to future payments (Cordilha 2022). Commercial health insurers pool their customers' savings for future health expenditure, apply financial techniques to premium payments to yield maximum profitability and to shift costs onto patients and employers, and engage in financial innovation and engineering new financial instruments such as high-deductible plans or MSAs that are described in Section 8 (Mulligan 2016; Karwowski 2019).

8 Contemporary Private Health Insurance Regimes

Of the three major financial sectors – banking, securities and insurance – insurance is the most closely related to the national economy, the livelihoods of normal people, China's fundamental policies, and our Chinese dream. Insurance is particularly relevant to people's lives.

'Insurance of the future. An interview with Ren Huichuan of Tencent'[24] (Chung 2021)

Insurance is best understood as a 'socio-political-economic technology' (McFall *et al.* 2020) as well as a financial technology. This final section of the volume brings a social science lens to the volume's account of private health insurance. Policy debates over the nature and extent of public insurance or the regulation of private insurance are almost always framed in economic terms (Baker 2000). These debates tend to focus on technical evaluation and the empirical evidence regarding the impact of private health insurance on health system performance, financial protection, access to health services, and efficiency and quality in health service organisation and delivery. The preceding sections have taken into account these issues and have also highlighted the political economy of the industry.

This section aims to demonstrate that the processes and societal influences of private health insurance are not only material but also ideational, and that this financial technology impacts social relations in fundamental ways. It is important to consider private health insurance's intimate interrelationship with commodification processes, social group differentiation, and inequalities.

A case study from South Africa will chart the industry's adaptive ability in the context of political change, its exploitation of ideas of 'inclusion', and how the instrument of the MSAs serves to reinforce the idea of the healthcare consumer. Section 8.1 then offers a case study of promotional marketing in India, highlighting its reliance on social differentiation and its relationship to class and consumption in the processes of demand creation. Section 8.2 explores how new digital technologies are facilitating the industry to perform overt and hidden regulatory activities in its day-to-day functioning and how digital innovation may also create new types of discrimination in the future. It is the contention of this Element that the combined socio-political-economic aspects of this financial technology constitute private health insurance *regimes*.

In the social sciences literature, insurance has generally been an underresearched institution, despite the sociological interest in risk. Indeed, McFall *et al.* (2020) remark that, for an industry of its size and governmental importance, this reveals the 'interestingly uninteresting' character of insurance. Within the small body of existing literature, important contributions on private health insurance in middle-income countries include the writings of the economic sociologist Ossandón on health insurance markets in Chile, which have been referred to in earlier sections (Ossandón 2014, 2015; Ossandón & Ureta 2019)

---

[24] Tencent's insurance-agency platform, WeSure, teams up with major domestic insurance companies to enable users to purchase insurance, make inquiries, and file claims through WeChat – a widely used messaging, social media, and payments application in China.

and an insightful special issue of Medical Anthropology Quarterly edited by Dao and Mulligan (Dao & Mulligan 2016).

These scholars particularly draw our attention to the twin processes of commodification and the destruction of societal obligations that take place through health insurance and related health reforms. Ossandón conceives of insurance as a type of economic good and draws on Science and Technology studies to highlight the performative role of the field of economics in turning things into economic objects or goods. For Ossandón, economics has been a key tool in building the insurance market. 'Economics works not like an ideology that is disseminated among economic agents, but rather as knowledge that is inscribed in tools used by economic actors to produce a calculable environment' (Ossandón 2015: 15).

Similarly, Dao and Mulligan emphasise that the growth of the commercial health insurance industry in the global South is taking place within a broader context of health economists' promotion of the technology of insurance within health systems, implementing a particular set of assumptions and ways of working (Dao & Mulligan 2016). The ideational influence of insurance is significant. Even at its most comprehensive, health insurance is based on individuals having a right to healthcare, rather than on the idea of societal obligation to look after the health of everyone (see also Light 2003). Furthermore, as ethnographic studies in Dao and Mulligan's collection illustrate, while social solidarity rhetoric is often part of the national discourses around health insurance reforms, the actual systems are more often embedded within neoliberal transformations of welfare states.

Pertinent sociological analyses beyond the health sphere include Ericson, Barry, and Doyle's extensive research on the private car, property, and life insurance industry in Canada, the United States, and Britain and their theory of insurance as governance (Doyle 2011; Ericson *et al.* 2000b; Ericson & Doyle 2006; Haggerty *et al.* 2004), also Finnish sociologists Lehtonen and Liukko (2010, 2011, 2015) on insurance solidarity. Most recently, McFall, with colleagues Meyer and Van Hoyweghen, has written on the adoption of Big Data analytics in insurance, an emerging topic returned to in Section 8.2 (McFall *et al.* 2020).

Ericson and colleagues (Doyle 2011; Ericson *et al.* 2000b) did not examine health insurance specifically, but they, too, were interested in how insurance reshapes responsibility among insured individuals and organisations. Indeed, for them, the private insurance industry is an ideal institution through which to examine neoliberalism as a model for governance beyond the state. They argue that insurance governs through a number of interconnected dimensions. Insurance companies interlock with other powerful corporations and the state to negotiate the political economy on all levels of society, and insurance also governs other institutions through its powers of transferring and distributing risks. It attempts to produce knowledge of risk by objectifying everything into degrees of chance of harm, and it makes everything it objectifies calculable and thereby subject to commodification.

In commercial insurance, actuarial techniques are used to create probability classifications, and each classification is then assigned its respective cost so that prices can be set and compensation for the effects of chance can be paid. Actuarialism creates a risk pool, a population that has a stake in the identified risks and the specific harms they entail, and this stake transforms the population into a collective with an interest in minimising loss and compensating those who have suffered loss (Doyle 2011; Ericson *et al.* 2000b). Similarly, Lehtonen and colleagues describe insurance as 'the economization of uncertainty' (Lehtonen & Liukko 2015; Lehtonen & Van Hoyweghen 2014). Uncertainty in itself has become a fundamental component of economic life, and when uncertainty is 'standardized, homogenized and made calculable' (Lehtonen and Van Hoyweghen 2014: 53), it can be given a price and can be bought and sold as a commodity.

Lehtonen and Van Hoyweghen (2014) note that the concrete ways in which insurance relations are practically arranged have an effect on the ways in which the related moral and political concepts of solidarity, inequality, and exclusion are perceived. So, what is solidarity for some can entail exclusion and inequality for others. This can be illustrated by what occurred in the aftermath of Türkiye's health financing reforms. Compulsory General Health Insurance (Genel Sağlık Sigortası) was rolled out from 2008, and the three existing public health insurance schemes and the green card scheme were united, removing some previous inequities. But at the same time, a new financing model introduced some additional financing mechanisms: con-tributory payments for hospital visits and medication, and additional pay-ments for private hospital visits (Yilmaz 2013). The industry now had the opportunity to expand the size of the commercial health insurance market. It could promote supplementary voluntary private health insurance to cover those additional payments for healthcare services and medications when the subscriber used one of the private hospitals offering services for the publicly insured (Erdoğan 2020). Effectively, this offered the better-off the ability to differentiate themselves from those on a low income by using more exclusive hospitals (Yilmaz 2013).

As expectations and aspirations in the population became redefined by this situation, supplementary insurance for their members became a demand from major trade unions in collective bargaining processes. Indeed, according to the chairman of the Turkish Employers' Association of the Metal Industries (MESS), the inclusion of supplementary voluntary private health insurance for their members represented 'new generation unionism' (quoted in Erdoğan 2020). Lavinas describes a similar ideational shift in Brazil, where 'the logic of privatisation is ingrained into society as a whole' (Lavinas 2017: 137) and has the support of a large flank of the trade union movement, which came to demand private healthcare plans as an indirect benefit for salaried employees and their families whenever negotiating with corporations or the State.

Social group differentiation and inclusion have both played a role in the market expansion of private health insurance. From 2011 to 2019, the global middle-class population was said to have increased from 899 million to 1.34 billion, or by 54 million people annually, on average, until the pandemic temporarily halted this growth (Kochhar 2021). By 2018, half of the world's population had enough disposable income to be classified by influential economists as middle class[25] or wealthy. For some, their newfound status was immensely vulnerable, and they could be suddenly pushed back into poverty by loss of income or catastrophic healthcare costs (Krishna 2011). But termed by some as the 'consumer class', the new middle class was contributing to national economic growth, experiencing pervasive economic indebtedness in new ways, and buying refrigerators, washing machines, smart phones, and insurance.

Perhaps even more than other types of insurance, commercial health insurance is intricately tied up with issues of social differentiation. Access to private insurance has come to be perceived by many as an indicator of improvement in their economic status and a marker of their social mobility. This, in turn, removes a collective interest in achieving high-quality care in the public services, replacing this with individualised ambitions to secure healthcare in the private sector for one's family. The commercial insurance industry supports the private healthcare sector with reliable income streams and contributes further to this social segmentation.

South Africa's trajectory is an exemplar of how the private health insurance industry adapts to social and political change, and also reinforces social inequalities over time. It has made its way through the exclusionary politics of apartheid, exploited a new era of 'financial inclusion' and moved on to create new instruments fitted to contemporary forms of segmentation by economic class. The country has a history of over a century of private health insurance arrangements, although only in 1967 did the Medical Schemes Act recognise and regulate the mutual health insurers. Health insurance cover was provided mainly by employer or industry-specific medical schemes, so-called 'closed funds'. Individual or small-group enrolment was only possible in 'open' funds, which became significant players in the early 1980s (Soderlund and Hansl 2000).

---

[25] See Reeves *et al.* (2018) and others for a discussion of the various cash /credentials /culture definitions of 'middle class'.

Before the 1970s, private health insurance only covered white workers, and political change and the end of apartheid were key drivers of the marketisation of commercial insurance for the poor in South Africa (Bähre 2016). This occurred at a time when, as Rose (1999) has described, the ideal of the 'social state' was giving way to that of the 'enabling state', one that empowered entrepreneurial subjects of choice in their self-realisation. 'Financial inclusion' was one of the central policies of the post-apartheid government as laid down in the Reconstruction and Development Programme. South African insurance companies duly expanded their business to include the black population, providing access to those working as domestic workers, security guards, or lower-ranking civil servants (Bähre 2016). Consolidating all these efforts, the Financial Sector Charter on Black Economic Empowerment came into effect in 2004, which, among other action areas, aimed to make it easier for the poor to access financial services.

Bähre (2012) described how all major South African insurers established specific departments to intensify their marketing to the poor and the lower middle classes, opening up offices in the townships and hiring local brokers from these areas. He found that in two townships in Cape Town, about three-quarters of residents had an insurance policy of some kind and that some had as many as nine policies, each often covering a very limited number of risks. Predominant among these were funeral policies, endowment plans, retirement annuities, and an insurance that covered the cost of schooling for children or grandchildren. Companies had to find ways to cut operational costs and make insurance affordable to the poor and profitable to the company, so brokers' income was based on commission from the products they sold, creating a temptation for brokers to missell. Bähre tells an emblematic story of an illiterate man living in a township in Cape Town who thought he had bought a comprehensive health policy, including ambulance transportation to the hospital. But when he became sick, it turned out that he had been sold a funeral policy (Bähre 2012: 153).

On top of these new marketing opportunities and in line with the rise of economic liberalisation ideologies, the industry benefited from government deregulation that took place in the mid-1980s (Soderlund & Hansl 2000). Up until 1989, health insurers had been required by law to 'community rate' their premiums and were not allowed to exclude high-risk enrolees from coverage. Schemes were forbidden from charging differential premiums based on the risk of ill health and were required by law to cover a certain percentage of the nationally mandated fee schedule for all healthcare provided. But in 1989, these regulations were removed, effectively allowing health insurers to risk-rate the coverage that they provided and exclude 'medically uninsurables' (Soderlund and Hansl 2000).

Today, the health insurance profile in South Africa is one of segmentation by economic class. Commercial health insurance offers access to private health-care providers for a relatively wealthy minority (16 per cent of the population), while the majority (84 per cent) rely on publicly financed services in public facilities. The magnitude of spending through private health insurance (about 47 per cent of total spending on health) significantly limits the potential for cross-subsidies in the healthcare system to benefit the poor or chronically sick (Thomson *et al.* 2020b: 29).

About 45 per cent of those with private health insurance in South Africa have MSAs. The MSA is a financial instrument that demonstrates the influence of the broader insurance industry on the overall narrative, moving it ever further away from pooled risk and toward individualised 'consumer-driven' or 'consumer-directed' healthcare cover, along with new life insurance and retirement designs (McLeod & McIntyre 2020). The argument given is that individual consumers need to take charge of purchasing healthcare goods and services because they will be more 'price-sensitive' in this situation. The primary policy vehicle advocated is the medical or health savings account coupled with a high-deductible insurance policy for serious conditions (Jost 2005). Probably influenced by Singapore's model, China has pursued a mandatory Health Savings Account for urban populations. In South Africa as in the USA, voluntary MSA models are offered.

MSAs were first introduced by the Discovery Health Medical Scheme in South Africa in 1994. Other schemes rapidly followed suit. Medical savings accounts allow healthy people to retain their tax-subsidised insurance payments as a form of savings, to which they can have access to pay for services not necessarily covered by medical schemes (private health insurance). Contributions from employers and employees are deducted before tax (McLeod and McIntyre 2020). The schemes also allow the healthy insured to defer taxes on their account balances until the time that they are withdrawn, possibly until retirement. Thus, as Jost (2005) has argued, the role of MSAs in South Africa was to provide medical schemes and their administrators,[26] who were becoming increasingly constrained by a restrictive re-regulating environment, with an ingenious and effective tool for risk selection.

---

[26] Although in South Africa all medical schemes (private health insurance schemes) are by law non-profit organisations, their administration is typically contracted out to a professional administration company that collects premiums, processes claims, contracts with providers, etc. While the mutual insurer model still largely applies to employment-based funds, most open medical schemes operate effectively as for-profits, with the distinction between fund revenue surplus and administration fees being a largely artificial one (see Soderlund and Hansl 2000).

These MSAs are often sold alongside plans that offer bonuses in terms of access to a range of exclusive gyms and exotic holidays for the insured. Such policies are, of course, more attractive to young, healthy people than to the older or sicker, allowing self-selection to occur. And, as McLeod and McIntyre (2020) have highlighted, because they are personalised for the individual members and their dependents, MSAs undermine income and risk cross-subsidies even more than risk-pooled private insurance. They also allow insurance funds to avoid their responsibility for strategic purchasing.

8.1 Private Health Insurance and the Craft of Promotional Marketing

Insurance companies invest heavily in promotional marketing and other technologies of consumption to overcome disinterest and resistance. This usually involves some combination of 'explaining' their technical approach to risk, exploiting sentiment, and cultivating brand attachment (Jeanningros & McFall 2020). Much of the marketing speaks to – and exacerbates – anxieties about one's own future and that of loved ones, emphasising the personal responsibility to identify suitable financial protection.

> **Insure Love this Valentine's Day!**
> **5 Points to Consider while Buying Health Insurance.**
> This Valentine's Day gift your partner a health insurance. The aim is to provide your partner the necessary financial security in the unfortunate event of a health crisis and mounting bills. This becomes a very thoughtful Valentine's gift since we are living in a pandemic-afflicted world, where we are witnessing harsh repercussions of medical emergencies. In such a scenario, health insurance is an indispensable pre-requisite of a modern life.
>
> (Business Desk News18 2022)

India, the recipient of this Valentine's Day advice, is a revealing example of how the news media construct the narrative around health and healthcare. Sometimes, this has been a narrative by omission, as Dreze and Sen pointed out in their 2013 book, *An Uncertain Glory, India and its Contradictions*. At that time, the subject of health was conspicuous by its absence in the press media (Dreze & Sen 2013). But now, the mood music is rather different. Almost every day, there is a 'news' explainer about how to choose a private health insurance plan, or what the business prospects are for the industry.

Bourdieu and Wacquant (2001) have highlighted how the logic of neo-liberalism is articulated, disseminated, and embedded in the social psyche through the perpetual repetition of neoliberal ideas in the news media. The readership of English-language dailies in India has historically consisted of the English-speaking elites, including policymakers and the educated urban middle class. Economic liberalisation in the 1990s contributed to the rapid commercialisation of the Indian news business (Rao 2010). There was also a disproportionate expansion of print and online niche market business news. As well as four national daily English-language economic newspapers there were regional and national supplements on business news in virtually all major newspapers, plus dozens of national business news magazines. Almost all of these had online counterparts (Chakravartty & Schiller 2010).

Journalists find themselves under immense pressure to appease corporate customers who lobby for advertorials aimed at the middle-class consumer (Rao 2010). The inventive advertorial on insurance as a Valentine's Day gift, was featured on News18.com, the online arm of CNN News18, which is a partnership between TV18, one of India's leading television broadcast networks and CNN International, the international news brand. Its stated aim is to 'provide the discerning viewers with a complete commitment to the needs and aspirations of the Indian viewer' (CNN-News18, no date).

The health insurance industry uses a number of techniques to place its products in the digital news media, to then be easily identified by search engines. There are many explainer blogs with syndicated feeds that are auto-generated and given a new headline and picture by the newspaper staff. Other 'brand posts' in online news media, such as the Hindustan Times, Economic Times, and Financial Express, are presented as informative articles but with a disclaimer at the bottom of the page stating, 'This is a company press release. No HT journalist is involved in the creation of this content'. These 'articles' are intended to serve several interrelated functions under the guise of providing the reader with better information.

The first function of such material is to raise anxiety and awareness of health risks:

> **Choose a comprehensive policy to cover COVID-induced diseases**
> On the surface, it might look like you need to protect yourself against COVID-19 and its variants. However, the past two years have taught us to tread with caution. COVID makes way for other diseases like hypertension, diabetes, obesity and heart ailments, among many others . . . Apart from that, you also need to protect yourself from other complications like black fungus. The consequences arising out of these could be severe and may even require hospitalisation.
>
> Extract from 'How to Make Your Health Insurance Policy Omicron-ready' in the *Financial Express*. (Chhabra 2021)

The second function is to raise concerns about the high costs of medical care:

> you also need to take due note of the upsurging medical inflation year after year. The second wave still serves as a dreadful reminder of how important it is to stay prepared in advance. The medical bills during this time have gone as high as Rs 85 lakh to Rs 1 crore. If you have an insufficient sum insured, you will end up paying the remaining amount. Especially in metro cities, these expenses can cut deep into your savings. (Chhabra 2021)

But, at the same time, the aim is to portray the health insurance industry as responsible and a particular company as being a reliable and authoritative source on subjects such as 'Omicron Scare: What Kind of Health Insurance Should You Buy For Your Parents?' (Maiti 2021). Frequently, the explainer articles and blogs are attributed to named industry CEOs, and provide direct links within the article to their firm or product websites and premium calculators. It's an 'industry of risk' that seeks out and creates markets for products in the interests of its own profit (Rose 1999).

The third function is to emphasise the personal responsibilities of heads of households, parents, children, and partners to care for loved ones or care for themselves through the purchase of health insurance products. For example, young people are exhorted to 'invest in yourself' in pieces such as 'Personal Finance: Understanding the importance of buying health insurance at a young age' (Chaphekar 2022) and 'Trends in financial planning among Gen Z and why adding insurance is a must do!' (Deshpande 2022).

For this audience, the tax advantages are highlighted, and finance terms are employed to emphasise that taking health insurance is part of the modern Indian's 'personal finances':

> Health insurance is purchased to hedge health risks which can affect anyone. But certain groups of individuals, irrespective of their current fitness and health, stand to gain a lot by investing in a suitable health insurance. These include those with a family history of susceptibility to certain ailments, women of childbearing age, individuals residing in zones of frequent communicable diseases, and frequent fliers or those in occupations with a higher propensity for disease exposure.
>
> Extract from 'Why health insurance is a must for some' a feature in the *Hindu Business Line* (Yadavalli 2022).

Special products are designed to fit the lifestyle aspirations of young middle-class Indians. For example, a group insurance plan with Care Health Insurance is initially available to homebuyers in a newly launched 'value housing project', the Mahindra Happinest Kalyan 2 in the Mumbai Metropolitan Region (Live Mint 2022). The Mahindra Lifespaces are housing complexes with 14-storey towers with green technology and facilities such as a jogging and cycling track and a rooftop lounge, 'crafted to take care of your physical, mental, and social fitness' (Mahindra Lifespaces 2022). The boost to mental health is offered by access to family health insurance, rope wall yoga, camping, and stargazing.

In the same vein, there are often appeals to notions of 'empowerment': 'The product has been launched to empower Indian women with good health and finances . . . Women are more susceptible to illnesses related to heart, gestation, reproduction, cancer and even hypertension and depression when compared to men' (Press Trust of India 2021).

For younger, more confident audiences, the advertising does not always have to appeal to anxieties but can speak to the new consumption patterns. The exuberant TV commercials for another product launched in 2021 were made by a well-known movie director. Concisely labelled 'fever', 'fracture' and 'cancer' they are described as showcasing 'how health insurance enables people to accumulate experiences and build memories' and they depict modern Indians who live full and adventurous lives before and after their medical treatment and related insurance claim.

In 'cancer', a bald-headed woman can be seen watching spectacular fireworks over the Eiffel Tower in Paris, while potential purchasers are urged to 'claim your life' (afaqs! news bureau 2021). The health insurance company has emphasised that the 'campaign is made with an intent to change the way health insurance is perceived by people': 'it aims to democratise health insurance in the country by positioning it as an enabler for living life the way it should be lived' (Economic Times 2021).

All opportunities, from Valentine's Day to World Cancer Day, are marketing opportunities, often emphasising the need for specialised and extra coverage.

> Cancer coverage is not eligible for those who have a pre-existing cancerous condition or are already impacted by cancer. Also, it does not cover skin cancer or sickness resulting from any congenital disease, biological, nuclear, or chemical contamination; contact with radiation or radioactivity from any non-diagnostic or therapeutic source cancer and those caused or contributed to by sexually transmitted diseases, HIV, or AIDS.
>
> Extract from 'All you need to know about cancer cover in health insurance' in the *Financial Express* (Chhabra 2022b)

There is encouragement for employers to take out insurance, for example, 'Why do small businesses need group health insurance' in the *Economic Times* (Garg 2021). And with around 8 million gig professionals in India and a rapidly growing gig economy, commercial health insurance is also devised with this new market in mind. For example, the AI-powered gig-work platform GigVistas, partnering with Alyve Health, offers health policy sign-up online to freelancers without prior medical check-up (Sarkar 2021). Plum, an employee health insurance platform, has also launched a product for this audience, Plum-Lite. This is advertised as providing 'comprehensive group health benefits membership exclusively for early-stage start-ups, SMEs and gig workers/freelance consultants' with 'new-age health insurance covers and doctor consultations', and COVID-19 treatment 'with a zero human touchpoint' (Live Mint 2021).

Online buying is a relatively new channel for insurance purchase in India, and until recently accounted for only 2 per cent of the market (Insurance Regulatory and Development Authority of India 2020). But as in China, it has taken off during the COVID-19 crisis as those beyond the circle working in and around IT have become accustomed to a new lifestyle with fewer face-to-face interactions.

Another underlying theme of these many blogs and advertorials is that enough is never quite enough. They work to normalise the idea that multiple plans will be needed and that more coverage will need to be purchased, as in this example from the *Financial Express*:

> Nowadays it is common for people to have multiple health insurance policies such as corporate, individual plan, family floater plan, critical illness, top-up plan and super top-up plans. (Sinha 2021)

Different articles encourage people to 'port' their policies or, conversely, to lock themselves into the system with a multi-year plan, as in a piece on 'Multiple benefits of upgrading to a multi-year health insurance' in the *India Express* (Chhabra 2022a).

Underpinning all of these is a moral discourse of insurance that emphasises the duty and responsibility of the citizen or head of the family to take out cover (Ellison 2014). The message is that if one chooses well, one can acquire the safety and certainty of good healthcare and financial protection. But the responsibility is personal. Prospective purchasers are even advised to take on the responsibility of checking the financial viability of the insurance company themselves:

> If you want to buy a health insurance policy, one of the factors you should look into is the solvency ratio of the insurer. This ratio will help determine your insurer's ability to repay the amount when you make a claim. According to IRDA guidelines, all companies are required to maintain a solvency ratio of 150 percent to minimise bankruptcy risk. Solvency ratio helps identify whether the company has enough financial buffer to settle all claims. Kulkarni (2022) in the *Economic Times*

The potential market for health insurance is huge in India, and it is not only the professional middle class who are receiving attention. The government think-tank NITI Aayog produced a report in 2021 on the health insurance 'space'. This emphasised the 30 per cent of the population devoid of state or private health insurance and termed this 'the missing middle' (Sarwal & Kumar 2021). This segment is predominantly the self-employed informal sector (agriculture and non-agriculture) in rural areas and the informal, semi-formal, and formal workers in urban areas. Efforts are also being made to engage with these sectors by using different distribution channels, as well as by applying zonal premiums to reflect the differing income levels of potential customers in different parts of the country.

As in the South African case, agents are the oldest channel of insurance sales in India, and these are still considered to be key to reaching the 'missing middle'. Amongst various channels for the distribution of health insurance policies, individual agents contributed a major share in the total health insurance premium at 35 per cent, according to the IRDA annual report 2020–1 (Insurance Regulatory and Development Authority of India 2020). In the individual health insurance premium sector, their share was as high as 74 per cent.

The same insurance company that produced 'fever' 'fracture' and 'cancer' for India's young middle classes is also embarking on what it terms a 'growth journey' expansion in southern India, seeking new clientele away from the mega cities, in Tier 3 and 4 towns,[27] with plans to hire 30,000 agents to sell policies there. Again, there is a hint at the empowering nature of insurance in this account from the Director of Health Insurance Retail Sales: 'We will provide adequate training programmes and encourage women and housewives in the southern market to become insurance agents, thereby helping them to become financially independent' (Businessline Bureau 2021).

'Bancassurance' is yet another distribution mechanism for commercial health insurance. Here, the bank is the channel for selling insurance products from their branches and using their existing customer resources and marketing. Care Health Insurance, for example, is offering products to farmers and artisans who are customers of the Gramin Bank, the regional rural bank network in Karnataka (BL Mangaluru Bureau 2021). As one bank is allowed to partner with only one insurance company, it offers little choice for customers, but it trades on the bank's reputation for reliability.

---

[27] Tier 3 towns had a population of 20,000–49,999 and Tier 4 had 10,000–19,999 at the time of the 2021 census.

Bancassurance is also considered to be a success in China, where people are acquainted with and have trust in banks. Therefore, bank services tend to be easily accepted (Wang 2009). In Brazil, to encourage the 'new' middle class to consume low-coverage healthcare plans, the federal government has been working directly through public banks such as Caixa Econômica Federal, which now offer highly segmented insurance as part of the newly expanding supplemental sector (Lavinas 2017).

8.2 Data Technologies and Hidden Regulation by Health Insurance

The picture is one of ever-widening market penetration and increased embeddedness of private health insurance. This, in turn, should raise new preoccupations because of the regulatory activities that insurance performs in its day-to-day functioning.

Overt attempts at regulation can be seen in the attempts to control unruly medical practitioners and limit the costs of claim reimbursement, shifting the costs to patients. But there are other less visible activities. A largely under-recognised regulatory function performed by insurance companies is their role in shaping who gets to participate in healthcare markets. Insurers select which providers to empanel and which to exclude, adjudicating over provider participation in the insurer-funded marketplace. They then determine which users can access these providers and services, using demographic characteristics and user health information to calculate risks and required premiums. Insurance manages that risk through surveillance:

> The increasing digitization of financial flows creates opportunities to accelerate progress. This digital transformation generates vast quantities of data about provider and patient behaviors. When systems are interoperable and connected, data can be harnessed to detect fraud and corruption, enhance transparency and accountability, and improve the design of pooling and especially purchasing policies. (World Bank 2019)

The new techniques and product innovations of 'connected insurance' have greatly enhanced the capacity for surveillance (Silvello & Procaccini 2019). Now, middle-income countries are part of a flourishing 'insurtech' market, in which the digital tech industries contribute to insurance practice and delivery through mobile apps, big data, and AI.

Indian health insurance apps include Religare Health and Star Power, as well as the PhonePe digital payments company app, which offers 'affordable' health insurance and also 'super top-up' plans. Ping An Health is the best-known health insurance app in China. Some apps simply allow customers to deal more efficiently with their documents by digitalising previously paper-based processes. Others, however, are based on the monitoring of individual behaviour and the sharing of health-related personal information. In the commodification of health regimes, health data are becoming increasingly valuable assets.

Wearables are seen as a 'non-invasive' underwriting evidence source, thanks to their capacity to collect data and assess risk based on this data. They can be used in marketing campaigns designed to boost engagement or create product differentiation. Linked to insurance, they can also be used to encourage people to improve their lifestyles and habits. For example, in India, Aditya Birla Health has led the field in offering discounts for policyholders who record a specified number of steps using an activity tracker, attend gym sessions, or have a health assessment (Gupta 2017). Proponents argue that offering wearables to insurance customers can help boost customer engagement through more regular contact 'helping the insurer to play a positive role in the lives of their policyholders' (Spender *et al.* 2019).

Discovery Limited's Vitality insurance programme has been a leader in the health field for the new 'connected insurance' and it claims to run 'the world's largest behaviour change programme linked to insurance' (Vitality 2021). Discovery was a South African start-up that quickly grew into a global player with a market capitalisation of over \$8 billion. The financial services group operates across the healthcare, life assurance, short-term insurance, savings and investments, banking, and wellness markets. The extent of its influence was indicated by the appointment of Vitality's founder and CEO to the World Economic Forum's Global Health Advisory Board in 2009.

Discovery's innovative health-insurance model 'that would make people healthier' began in South Africa in 1992 in response to a regulatory environment that did not permit the rating of customers on pre-existing conditions. The company has elaborated a system of value-based practices and a socio-economic philosophy to support its 'Shared Value Insurance' (Jeanningros & McFall 2020). It uses cashback for healthy food purchases and gym membership to incentivise healthier lifestyle choices, asserting that 'we can deliver economic and health benefits that are good for our members as well as intermediaries, for us as a business and good for society' (Vitality 2021).

With 20 million users by 2019, Vitality is now operating in thirty-six countries. The flexibility of the organisation's structure allows it to engage in markets that Discovery would have difficulty entering as the main insurer. Instead, it partners with established insurers in those markets and these integrate Vitality into their platforms. There are plans to roll out group insurance to employers in five countries in the African continent (Vitality Health International Press Release 2022). Business is also booming in the Asia Pacific. Among other partnerships,

Discovery has had an equity stake in Ping An Health, working with one of China's largest insurers, Ping An (Gore 2015).

The Vitality programme has a common core around three main phases that are customised locally: behavioural assessment, improvement, and reward. The initial stage includes standard health assessment tests combined with the Vitality Health Review of individual nutrition and wellness habits, vaccinations, dental and cancer screenings. Based on these reviews, customers are advised of their 'Vitality age' presented as a 'scientific calculation' (see Jeanningros & McFall 2020). It then uses loyalty and behaviour modification programmes via a reward system and gamification to keep clients engaged.

The programme attracts younger and healthier people because, in many countries, it is these individuals who are comfortable with technological, more digital insurance. Subscribers can complete online health assessments to understand their health risks and receive weekly goals to increase their physical activity levels and earn rewards with Vitality. The gamification strategy is run with the support of an extended network of partners. Vitality customers earn points by logging their workouts with fitness devices from Nike+, Fitbit, and others, and these sync-up with Vitality directly through mobile apps. Mini challenges related to shopping for food, physical and sporting activities, and medical check-ups are rewarded with cashback, discounts, or other types of incentives. There are incentives for customers not only to meet behavioural targets but also to share their data with the company and to share their progress on social media. This sharing assists the commercial performance of the business both in the technical valuation of risk and by enhancing the sentimental appeal of the brand (Jeanningros & McFall 2020).

Despite the enthusiasm with which such programmes are often met, this can be seen as problematic on several counts. As Prainsack (2020) has pointed out in her critique of 'nudge' interventions in healthcare, the idea of changing the 'choice architecture' of people hinges on the assumption that individuals can freely choose what they do and draws attention away from the larger structural elements that shape people's practices. In contrast to solidarity, which emphasises interdependencies with others (Prainsack & Buyx 2014, 2017), the underpinning is an individualistic ontology that treats people as ideally bounded, atomised, independent, and 'rational' entities. But more than this, the datafication[28] and digitalisation implicit in these programmes and in others offer new opportunities for data mining, and possibly for algorithmic predictions.

---

[28] Prainsack (2020) delineates datafication as referring to the phenomenon that ever wider aspects of our bodies and lives that used to remain private are now recorded (typically, but not necessarily, by digital means) and digitalisation as moving things and practices from the analogue to the digital domain.

The use of connected devices in its Vitality programme gives Discovery precious data on people's lifestyle and health conditions, and it is said to have been investing heavily in analytics for several years (Jacobs 2017). In December 2021, Discovery issued a press release giving 'real-world' information on the Omicron outbreak based on 211,000 positive test cases and collaboration with the South African Medical Research Council on ascertaining vaccine effectiveness (Science Media Centre 2021). Such data use can easily be defended as demonstrating social value.

The commercial uses, however, are far less comforting. Data mining is a well-established practice in marketing, advertising, finance, banking, and insurance. Various techniques (classification, clustering, association rule mining, and summarisation) are used to discover trends within the data (Andrea *et al.* 2019). The new information generated can provide businesses with accurate 'profiles' of consumers, enabling them to target their customers more effectively. Predictive analysis and scenario-based modelling enable companies 'to devise customized solutions for their clientele at varied pricing options' (ResearchAndMarkets.com 2022). In insurance terms, this helps create a clearer segmentation and thus the ability to 'select risk' in a more effective way. It increases the potential for an insurance company to cherry-pick only those people who are healthy and require fewer health services.

However, beyond this, it is the use of algorithmic prediction in digital insurance that has the potential to radically change the future operation of private health insurance and its social consequences (Cevolino & Esposito 2020; McFall *et al.* 2020). As Cevolino and Esposito (2020) have elaborated, this could result in a move from the use of statistical risk pools to predictive personalised profiles.

Troublesome social category variables such as gender, age, race, or place of residence could be ostensibly replaced by behavioural variables, and insurance policies and premiums might be calculated directly based on individual behaviour and level of risk. In the individualistic lexicon of the contemporary world, this new technique of governance could be justified for reasons of 'fairness' or the idea that those who take more risks should pay more, rendering the social context of 'unhealthy' behaviours invisible. In the future, it may be personalisation of private health insurance policies that shapes life-chances and produces new forms of discrimination. It is quite possible that middle-income countries with market-favouring regulatory systems may become the testing grounds.

9 Final Observations

This volume is a contribution to unsettling what seems to have become taken-for-granted in healthcare and development policy. It sets out to explore and problematise the rationale and operation of commercial health insurance and to do so through an examination of its advance in middle-income countries. In order to elaborate a wider account, it has drawn on the experiences of five countries, three with a long history of private health insurance companies and two in which the industry is putting considerable effort and resources into developing new markets.

The case of Chile is pertinent because it allows one to take a longer look, in the temporal sense, at the overt 'market turn' in a middle-income country while recognising the particularities of context. It is a very clear example of the embedded nature of the market and of how a state actively hollowed itself out and invited health insurance companies in. Brazil tells us some important things about mixed economy regimes in healthcare in a period of financialisation of social policy, the entanglement of the industry and the state, and the role of private health insurance in sustaining social difference with state support. The South African industry has brought some of the inventive approaches to commercial health insurance into the world market, and the country has passed through disastrous industry deregulation, policies of financial inclusion for its Black and Mixed-race populations, and now attempts to roll back and re-regulate commercial health insurance with a view to a single National Health Insurance. China and India are considered to be the big markets of the future, and Section 8.1 gives an illustration of how the industry uses technologies of consumption to develop demand, adapting its offer with ease to new conditions in the contemporary world including the gig economy.

In both India and China, it has been state support for the development of the broader insurance industry that has led to health insurance development. And in both cases, governments have accepted commercial health insurance as an important funding source for the private hospital sector and a means to lessen pressure on public services. However, healthcare plans with broad, truly adequate coverage are only accessible to a small elite. In many populous countries, including India, South Africa, and Brazil, new markets have been created by the 'innovation' of highly restricted plans destined for lower income groups (Bahia *et al.* 2016a). In practice, people taking out such plans are often unaware of the actual degree of coverage they will be entitled to, and what will be exempt in the event that they need it.

The integration of commercial insurance companies as advisors, managers, and implementing agencies for state-subsidised private health insurance is a growing phenomenon. Working with the state in this way provides the industry with an opportunity to access population data for their market development. The global management consultancy firm McKinsey has urged insurance companies to 'Get smart about medical data' in China, arguing that 'the rollout of public insurance and reimbursement schemes is producing a trove of health-related data that could offer valuable insights into healthcare needs and risks'. Insurers were advised to start interacting with the Ministry of Human Resources and Social Security to explore 'ways to leverage these data in order to better understand the market and to shape the future of the data environment in China' (Ng *et al.* 2012: 81).

In India, the urging came from the federal government's own policy think tank, NITI Aayog in its strategy document for the marketing of health insurance to the 'missing middle'. It has suggested the sharing of the data from the government schemes for subsidised food security, small farmers' assistance, and accidental death and disability insurance with the private health insurance industry in order to help ease the identification of, and outreach to, potential customers by insurers (Sarwal & Kumar 2021).

Private health insurance is a facilitative mechanism whereby profitable private healthcare services are provided through market relationships to those able to pay, and it is itself a focus of investment for profit. The actuarial nature of private insurance necessitates commodified healthcare and contributes to further commercialisation and commodification processes, adding new dimensions to the complexities of the dramatic spread of market relationships in the health sector of many middle-income countries in the last decades (Bloom *et al.* 2013).

Further than this, private health insurance shapes institutions and daily lives in ways that are largely invisible, bearing out Ericson *et al.*'s analysis of insurance as governance. Not only is the industry a significant player in the political economy, but despite the curious rhetoric of insurance as a form of solidarity, commercial health insurance – the way it is advertised, marketed, and conducted – is antisocial. It is based on a person's characteristics and aspirations, on their ability to make payments, on social distinction, on treating illnesses as individual rather than public health concerns, and on neoliberal notions of consumer choice.

Private health insurance constitutes fragmented and unequal communities of policyholders because commercial insurance has not been in the business of redistributing resources among the insured but rather of discriminating in favour of those who contribute to the 'goodness' of the pool and the prosperity of the company (Ericson *et al.*, 2000b). The 'insurtech' market now brings the industry potential new instruments for governance, including the possibilities of algorithmic prediction for the design of policies and the costing of premiums based on personalised behaviour profiles. These can be expected to feed into a moralising around individual responsibility and blame for the state of a person's well-being while making the structural causes of ill health ever more opaque.

Some may argue that health insurance companies are just doing their job as businesses, and as financial actors, in the modern world. But political philosophers like Michael J. Sandel and Deborah Satz are among the many who have raised the fundamental problems with letting market values crowd out non-market norms, as has occurred in almost every aspect of life. Sandel has argued against the drift from *having* a market economy to *being* a market society (Sandel 2012).

Satz has asked questions about the moral limits of markets, emphasising that these not only allocate resources and incomes but shape culture, foster or thwart human development, and create and support structures of power. She has argued that things should not be for sale if they come from weak agency or great vulnerabilities or if they produce bad outcomes for individuals or for society. This argument has considerable relevance to commercial health insurance and its associated markets, which, as this volume has tried to show, undermine the framework needed for a society of equals and prioritise and support powerful institutions that are largely unaccountable (Satz 2010).

It has become accepted discourse to refer to health systems as 'pluralistic' with 'complementary' sectors, and from there to focus on how the private for-profit elements may become better integrated. For examples, see Bloom *et al.* (2015) on addressing resistance to antibiotics; Drummond *et al.* (2022) on health technology assessment; Preker *et al.* (2021) on achieving UHC in middle-income countries. This type of narrative accommodates industries that can see opportunities to make money both in middle-class consumer markets and in outsourced government schemes and services.

It is also often reiterated that voluntary health insurance makes only a small contribution to spending on healthcare, as if it is therefore unimportant and with little influence. The experiences of the forerunner countries like Chile and Brazil, whose segmented access to healthcare is shaped by commercial health insurance, suggest differently. A private health insurance regime – one in which the power and practices of private health insurance shape *everyone's* experiences of healthcare and govern expectations and behaviours of governments and individuals – does not require a majority of health spend to be from private health insurance policies.

Chile's experience of the constitutional 'right' to choose and a substitutive system has been the most extreme, but in many ways, the stories elsewhere are not so different. Research by Brazilian scholars tells us that having a constitutional right to health is insufficient when the door is left open to commercial activity, and that supplementary insurance is far from being some simple backup to the public healthcare system. Insurance prices and redistributes risk, and it sits within a larger picture of new social identities based on consumption and credit.

For some, the status differentiation it affords is a driving factor, for others, the belief that private insurance may provide a route to a less dismal quality of care. This has altered the aspiration of populations, disabling the collective fight for improvement in public health services.

Contemporary private health insurance regimes reflect and actively recreate ideas about citizen rights and individualised responsibility. This is illustrated by the case studies of health insurance advertising in India, in new financial instruments such as the 'consumer-directed' MSAs, and in the behaviour modification programme from South Africa. The reshaping of responsibility is being enacted in the health sector in middle-income countries across the world. Exhorted to invest in themselves, citizens are required to weave together a basket of protection for their loved ones, often largely reliant on industry's advertorials for their information, and must bear individual responsibility for the nature and consequences of those choices.[29] By failing in the adequate provision of public healthcare services on the one hand, and by knowingly facilitating health insurance market development on the other, governments are complicit and responsible. This came brutally to the fore in the worldwide COVID-19 epidemic.

One of the ways in which health insurance has changed the relationship between citizens and the state is manifested in the growing judicialisation of healthcare, in which it becomes redefined as an issue of consumer rights. In Brazil, the most contested items are the restrictions in coverage, especially the most expensive and complex treatments, and courts find in favour of patients in over 90 per cent of these cases (Bahia *et al.* 2016a). In Chile, premium hikes were successfully contested in the courts. But as Abadía-Barrero's ethnographic work in Colombia demonstrates, while such victories can be celebrated, people's sense of justice in healthcare has been transformed. When citizens take legal actions to obtain reimbursements for services, this has broader implications for moral notions of justice. Healthcare is no longer understood through the 'right to life' but about having 'rights in life'. The right to healthcare has been privatised (Abadía-Barrero 2016).

Commercial insurance is currently portrayed by its advocates as the answer to overstretched public healthcare systems and obligations to meet the SDGs. So it is

---

[29] Online crowd funding of complex medical treatments through platforms such as Ketto is gaining popularity in India and China. While this might, at first glance, seem to be a challenge to the individualising nature of the commercial insurance model, it relies on benevolence and on individual citizens, rather than the state, taking responsibility, and it provides a new funding stream to the private hospital sector. It can also provide the insurance industry with opportunities to promote themselves to potential clients.

important to reiterate that the promotion of commercial health insurance is part of a wider financialisation of the health sector, a mechanism whereby financial interests can pursue penetration and new market growth. Encouraged by development banks, states all too often facilitate market development, integrate private voluntary health insurance into the design of their health system financing, and welcome the investment income from insurance funds.

Growth in the commercial health insurance sector often complements policies aimed at reducing welfare state healthcare provision to a safety net role, as well as the increased contracting-out of public sector healthcare provision to private sector providers. Importantly, over time, the 'multi-pillar' health system becomes increasingly unbalanced as resources drain further toward private sector healthcare provision and the opportunities for wealth accumulation that this offers.

For Ericson and colleagues, the private insurance industry is an ideal institution through which to examine neoliberalism as a model for governance beyond the state (Ericson *et al.* 2000b). Chile, under military dictatorship, was an early laboratory for Friedman's neoliberal ideas about the economy. China has taken a very different route, but the drive for economic development and the reincorporation into world trade agreements has reinstated the influence of mainstream economics on leadership decisions about reforms in the health and other sectors (Weber 2020). China too has become part of the global economy and the neoliberal order. Lavinas, in her clear eyed and angry book on the 'Brazilian paradox', has described in detail Brazil's decline from initially resisting the neoliberal wave to a situation where the developmentalist state wound up carrying out the task of the seizure of social policy through a variety of policies, programs, regulations, and finance-friendly deregulation:

> Instead of resisting the logic of finance, the social protection system becomes a new frontier by which finance may disseminate new devices for risk management and mitigation, rendering the institutions and mechanisms that made it possible to prevent risks and cope with uncertainty through a risk-sharing system based on progressive taxes and social security schemes increasingly obsolete. (Lavinas 2017: 172)

Across the world, financial markets, actors, institutions, and technologies are increasingly determining which kinds of services and 'Welfare' are provided (Stein & Sridhar 2018), how these are provided, and with what underlying assumptions. Private health insurance is just one of numerous socio-political-economic technologies in the contemporary era, but a close examination of private health insurance regimes can be revelatory of the forms of governance to which we are subjected and of what comes to be accepted in the 'common sense' of people's daily lives.

Abbreviations

AFP	Administradoras de Fondos de Pensiones
AFJP	Administradoras De Fondos De Jubilaciones Y Pensiones
AI	Artificial Intelligence
AIG	American International Group, Inc.
AIU	American International Underwriters
ANS	National Agency of Supplementary Health
AUGE	Acceso Universal de Garantías Explícitas
CEO	Chief Executive Officer
CIRC	China Insurance Regulatory Commission
CNSeg	National Confederation of General Insurance, Private Pensions and Life, and Supplementary Health and Capitalization
CNY	Chinese Yuan
FNE	Fiscalía Nacional Económica
FONASA	Fondo Nacional de Salud
GATS	General Agreement on Trade in Services
GDP	Gross Domestic Product
IBRD	International Bank for Reconstruction and Development
IFC	International Finance Corporation
ILC	Inversiones La Construcción
ILO	International Labour Organisation
IRDA	Insurance Regulatory and Development Authority of India
ISAPRE	Instituciones de Salud Previsional
IT	Information Technology
MDGs	Millennium Development Goals
MESS	Association of the Metal Industries
MSA	Medical Savings Account
NITI	Aayog National Institution for Transforming India
OECD	The Organisation for Economic Co-operation and Development
OOP	Out of Pocket
P&C	Property and Casual
PHI	Private Health Insurance
RSBY	Rashtriya Swasthya Bima Yojana
SDGs	Sustainable Development Goals
SME	Small & Medium Enterprises
SUS	Sistema Único de Saúde
TPA	Third-Party Administrator

UHC	Universal Health Coverage
UHI	Universal Health Insurance
USAID	United States Agency for International Development
VPHI	Voluntary Private Health Insurance
WHO	World Health Organization
WTO	World Trade Organization

References

Abadía-Barrero, C. E. (2016). Neoliberal justice and the transformation of the moral: The privatization of the right to health care in Colombia. *Medical Anthropology Quarterly*, **30**(1), 62–79.

Abbasi, K. (1999). The World Bank and world health: Changing sides. *British Medical Journal*, **318**, 865–9.

Adlung, R. (2010). Trade in healthcare and health insurance services: WTO/GATS as a supporting actor (?). *Intereconomics*, **45**(4), 227–38.

Afaqs! News Bureau. (2021). Max Bupa Health Insurance rebrands to Niva Bupa Health Insurance, launches new ad campaign. *Afaqs!*, 29 November. www.afaqs.com/news/advertising/max-bupa-health-insurance-rebrands-to-niva-bupa-health-insurance-launches-ad-campaign.

Agostini, C. A. , Saavedra, E. H., & Willington, M. M. (2008). Collusion in the Private Health Insurance Market: Empirical Evidence for Chile. May 16. https://ssrn.com/abstract=1149928 or http://dx.doi.org/10.2139/ssrn.1149928.

Almasi, T., Fasseeh, A. N., Elezbawy, B. et al. (2018). Role of supplementary and complementary private health insurance in selected countries. *Value in Health*, **21**, S180. Conference Abstract PHP178.

Alvarez, L., Salmon, W., & Swartzman, D. (2011). The Colombian health insurance system and its effect on access to health care. *International Journal of Health Services*, **41**(2), 355–70.

Andrea, M., Davida, S., & Simonea, E. B. (2019). Stay fit or get bit – ethical issues in sharing health data with insurers' apps. *Swiss Medical Weekly*, **149** (25–26), 1–8. https://doi.org/10.4414/smw.2019.20089.

Armada, F., Muntaner, C., & Navarro, V. (2001). Health and social security reforms in Latin America: The convergence of the World Health Organization, the World Bank, and transnational corporations. *International Journal of Health Services*, **31**(4), 729–68.

Asia Insurance Review. (2018). India: Complaints mount at 'headless' insurance Ombudsman offices. May. www.asiainsurancereview.com/Magazine/ReadMagazineArticle?aid=40875.

Asia Insurance Review. (2019). China: Insurance industry's total assets increase by 9.5%. 11 February. www.asiainsurancereview.com/News/View-NewsLetter-Article?id=45624&Type=eDaily.

Association of British Insurers. (2022). Insurers as investors. www.abi.org.uk/data-and-resources/tools-and-resources/regulation/insurers-as-investors/.

Bahia, L., Scheffer, M., Dal Poz, M., & Travassos, C. (2016a). Planos privados de saúde com coberturas restritas: Atualização da agenda privatizante no contexto de crise política e econômica no Brasil. *Cadernos de Saude Publica*, **32**(12), 8–12.

Bahia, L., Scheffer, M., Tavares, L. R., & Braga, I. F. (2016b). From health plan companies to international insurance companies: Changes in the accumulation regime and repercussions on the healthcare system in Brazil. *Cadernos de Saúde Pública*, **32**(Suppl 2), 1–18.

Bähre, E. (2012). The Janus face of insurance in South Africa: From costs to risk, from networks to bureaucracies. *Africa*, **82**(1), 150–67.

Bähre, E. (2016). Murder of gain: Commercial insurance and moralities in South Africa. In J. Wiegratz, & D. Whyte, eds., *Neoliberalism and the Moral Economy of Fraud*. Abingdon: Routledge, pp. 142–54.

Baker, T. (2000). Insuring morality. *Economy and Society*, **29**(4), 559–77.

Bartlett, J. (2022a). Misinformation abounds as Chile prepares to vote on new constitution. *The Guardian*, 31 August, London. www.theguardian.com/world/2022/aug/31/chile-new-constitution-vote-misinformation.

Bartlett, J. (2022b). Chile votes overwhelmingly to reject new, progressive constitution. *The Guardian*, 5 September, London. www.theguardian.com/world/2022/sep/05/chile-votes-overwhelmingly-to-reject-new-progressive-constitution.

Baru, R. V., & Nundy, M. (2020). *Commercialisation of Medical Care in China*. Oxford: Routledge.

BearingPoint. (2008). *Private Health Insurance in India: Promise and Reality*. Bengaluru: BearingPoint for USAID, 1–254.

Benoît, C., Del Sol, M., & Martin, P. (2021). The European Union, the Insurance Industry and the Public-Private Mix in Healthcare. In C. Benoît, M. Del Sol, & P. Martin, eds., *Private Health Insurance and the European Union*. Cham, Switzerland: Palgrave Macmillan.

Binder, S., & Mußhoff, J. (2017). *Global Insurance Industry Insights an In-depth Perspective, 7th ed.* McKinsey, 1–58.

Binder, S., Klais, P., & Mußhoff, J. (2021a). *2020 Global Insurance Pools Statistics and Trends: Nonlife Insurance*. McKinsey, 1–11.

Binder, S., Klais, P., & Mußhoff, J. (2021b). *Global Insurance Industry Insights, 9th ed.* McKinsey, 1–40.

Birch, K., & Siemiatycki, M. (2016). Neoliberalism and the geographies of marketization: The entangling of state and markets. *Progress in Human Geography*, **40**(2), 177–98.

Birn, A., & Nervi, L. (2019). What matters in health (care) universes: Delusions, dilutions, and ways towards universal health justice. *Globalization and Health*, **15**(Suppl 1), 1–12.

Birn, A., Nervi, L., & Siqueira, E. (2016). Neoliberalism redux: The global health policy agenda and the politics of cooptation in Latin America and beyond. *Development and Change*, **47**(4), 734–59.

BL Mangaluru Bureau. (2021). Karnataka Gramin Bank in pact with Care Health Insurance. *The Hindu Business Line*, 20 December, Mangalura. www.thehindubusinessline.com/money-and-banking/karnataka-gramin-bank-in-pact-with-care-health-insurance/article37995842.ece.

Bloom, G., Kanjilal, B., Lucas, H., & Peters, D. H. (2013). *Transforming Health Markets in Asia and Africa*. Abingdon: Routledge.

Bloom, G., Wilkinson, A., Tomson, G. et al. (2015). *Addressing Resistance to Antibiotics in Pluralistic Health Systems*, STEPS Working Paper No. 84, Brighton: STEPS Centre, 1–24.

Bloomberg. (2016). Chile's health insurers pushed to brink of collapse as courts prevent rate hikes. *Insurance Journal*, 12 August. www.insurancejournal.com/news/international/2016/08/12/423098.htm.

Bnamericas. (2019). At a glance: The main players in Brazilian health insurance. 9 August. www.bnamericas.com/en/news/at-a-glance-the-main-players-in-brazilian-health-insurance.

Borrescio-Higa, F., & Valdés, N. (2019). Publicly insured caesarean sections in private hospitals: A repeated cross-sectional analysis in Chile. *BMJ Open*, **9**, e024241. https://doi.org/10.1136/bmjopen-2018-024241.

Bourdieu, P., & Wacquant, L. (2001). NewLiberalSpeak: Notes on the new planetary vulgate. *Radical Philosophy*, **5**(105), 2–5.

Braveman, P., Starfield, B., & Geiger, H. J. (2001). World Health Report 2000: How it removes equity from the agenda for public health monitoring and policy. *BMJ*, **323**, 678–79.

Burns, D., Cowie, L., Earle, J. et al. (2016). *Where Does the Money Go? Financialised Chains and the Crisis in Residential Care*. CRESC Public Interest Report March 2016. University of Manchester & The Open University: Centre for Research on Socio-Cultural Change, 1–68.

Business Desk. (2022). Insure love this valentine's day: 5 points to consider while buying health insurance. *News18*, 13 February, India. www.news18.com/news/business/savings-and-investments/insure-love-this-valentines-day-5-points-to-consider-while-buying-health-insurance-4767257.html.

Businessline Bureau. (2021). Niva Bupa Health Insurance to hire 30,000 agents for South push. *The Hindu Business Line*, 22 December, Chennai.

www.thehindubusinessline.com/companies/niva-bupa-health-insurance-to-hire-30000-agents-for-south-push/article38015290.ece.

Cacace, M., & Schmid, A. (2008). Explaining convergence and common trends in the role of the state in OECD healthcare systems. *Harvard Health Policy Review*, **9**(1), 5–16.

CareEdge. (2021). *Health Insurance – Bright Spot amidst the Pandemic Blues*. Mumbai: CareEdge (Care Group), 1–6. www.careratings.com/uploads/news files/17122021060958_Health_Insurance_-_Bright_spot_amidst_the_Pandemic_Blues.pdf.

CEIC. (2022). *China Insurance Industry: Total Asset*. Beijing: China Banking and Insurance Regulatory Commission. www.ceicdata.com/en/china/insurance-industry-balance-sheet/cn-insurance-industry-total-asset.

Cevolini, A., & Esposito, E. (2020). From pool to profile: Social consequences of algorithmic prediction in insurance. *Big Data & Society*, **7**(2), 1–11.

Chakrabarty, A. (2020). Covid-19 fear makes people rush for health insurance cover. *The Financial Express*, June. www.financialexpress.com/money/insurance/covid-19-fear-makes-people-rush-for-health-insurance-cover/1999345/.

Chakravartty, P., & Schiller, D. (2010). Neoliberal newspeak and digital capitalism in crisis. *International Journal of Communication*, **4**, 670–92.

Chaphekar, S. (2022). Personal finance: Understanding the importance of buying health insurance at a young age. *The Free Press Journal*, 23 January. www.freepressjournal.in/business/personal-finance-understanding-the-importance-of-buying-health-insurance-at-a-young-age.

Chee, H. L. (2007). Medical tourism in Malaysia: International movement of healthcare consumers and the commodification of healthcare. *SSRN Electronic Journal*, ARI Working Paper No. 83. Singapore: Asia Research Institute, 1–3.3.

Chekh, E. L. (2020). Planes de mujeres en isapres subieron tras circular que prohibió contratos 'sin útero'. *La Tercera*, 13 January. www.latercera.com/nacional/noticia/planes-mujeres-isapres-subieron-tras-circular-prohibio-contratos-sin-utero/971314/.

Chen, H., & Lin, Y. (2012). Waiting for the boom: Helen Chen and Yanyan Lin of L.E.K. Consulting examine China's nascent private health insurance market. www.lek.com/insights.

Chen, N., Bai, J., Nicholas, S. et al. (2022). Preferences for private health insurance in China: A discrete choice experiment. *Frontiers of Public Health*, **10**, 985582. https://doi.org/10.3389/fpubh.2022.98558.

Chhabra, A. (2021). How to make your health insurance policy Omicron-ready. *The Financial Express*, 19 December. www.financialexpress.com/money/

insurance/how-to-make-your-health-insurance-policy-omicron-ready/ 2383361/.

Chhabra, A. (2022a). Multiple benefits of upgrading to a multi-year health insurance. *The Indian Express*, 13 January. https://indianexpress.com/art icle/business/the-multiple-benefits-of-upgrading-to-a-multi-year-health-insurance-7721274/.

Chhabra, A. (2022b). All you need to know about cancer cover in health insurance. *Financial Express*, 4 February. www.financialexpress.com/ money/all-you-need-to-know-about-cancer-cover-in-health-insurance/ 2425699/.

Chiang, L. (2008). China lets insurers invest in non-listed firms. *Reuters*, 7 November, Beijing.

China Daily. (2006). Regulator opens up banks to insurers. 13 June. http:// english.china.org.cn/english/BAT/171231.htm.

Chung, V. (2021). Insurance of the future: An interview with Ren Huichuan of Tencent. *McKinsey's Insurance Industry Leaders and Shapers*, 16 December. www.mckinsey.com/industries/financial-services/our-insights/insurance-of-the-future-an-interview-with-ren-huichuan-of-tencent.

Chung, V., Ho, B., Ho, D., & Roth, M. (2020). Industrializing data and analytics among Asian insurers. *McKinsey & Company Insurance Insights That Matter Blog*, July. www.mckinsey.com/industries/financial-services/our-insights/ insurance-blog/industrializing-data-and-analytics-among-asian-insurers.

Cid, C., Torche, A., Bastías, G., Herrera, C., & Barrios, X. (2013). Bases para una Reforma Necesaria al Seguro Social de Salud Chileno. In Pontificia Universidad Católica de Chile, ed., *Propuestas Para Chile*. Santiago de Chile: CPP-UC, pp. 183–220.

Clínicas de Chile. (2022). Dimensionamiento del sector de salud privado en Chile CIFRAS AL AÑO 2020, Santiago. 1–35. Retrieved from https://www.clinicasde chile.cl/wp-content/uploads/2022/04/Resumen-Ejecutivo-Dimensionamiento_ compressed.pdf.

CNN-News18. (no date). About News18. www.news18.com/about_us.php.

Collucci, C. (2016). Universal access to healthcare should be reconsidered, says Brazil's new health minister. *Folha de São Paulo*, 17 May. www.folha.uol .com.br/internacional/en/brazil/2016/05/1772048-universal-access-to-health care-should-be-reconsidered-says-brazils-new-health-minister.shtml.

Connell, J. (2013). Contemporary medical tourism: Conceptualisation, culture and commodification. *Tourism Management*, **34**, 1–13.

Cooperativa.cl. (2022). Corte Suprema ordenó suspender alza de planes anuales de isapres. 18 August. www.cooperativa.cl/noticias/pais/salud/isapre/corte-suprema-ordeno-suspender-alza-de-planes-anuales-de-isapres/2022–08-18/ 173459.html.

Cordilha, A. C. (2022). *Public Health Systems in the Age of Financialization: Lessons from France and Brazil*, Thesis de Doctorat, Université Sorbonne Paris Nord.

Crispi, F., Cherla, A., Vivaldi, E. A., & Mossialos, E. (2020). Rebuilding the broken health contract in Chile. *The Lancet*, **395**(10233), 1342.

Dao, A. (2018). *The Social Life of Health Insurance Temporality, Care, and the Politics of Financing Health in Rural Vietnam*. https://academiccommons .columbia.edu/doi/10.7916/D8127946.

Dao, A., & Mulligan, J. (2016). Toward an anthropology of insurance and health reform: An introduction to the special issue. *Medical Anthropology Quarterly*, **30**(1), 5–17.

Deacon, B. (2007). *Global Social Policy and Governance*. London: SAGE.

Deloitte. (2019). Global health care sector outlook: Shaping the future. *Deloitte Report*, London.

Deshpande, S. (2022). Trends in financial planning among Gen Z and why adding insurance is a must-do! *The Financial Express*, 9 February. www .financialexpress.com/money/trends-in-financial-planning-among-gen-z-and-why-adding-insurance-is-a-must-do/2429341/.

Dieleman, J. L., Campbell, M., Chapin, A. et al. (2017). Future and potential spending on health 2015–40: Development assistance for health, and government, prepaid private, and out-of-pocket health spending in 184 countries. *The Lancet*, **389**(10083), 2005–30.

Doyle, A. (2011). Introduction: Insurance and business ethics. *Journal of Business Ethics,* Special issue on Insurance and Business Ethics, **103**, 1–5.

Drechsler, D., & Jütting, J. (2005a). *Is there a Role for Private Health Insurance in Developing Countries?*, DIW Discussion Papers No. 517, Berlin: Deutsches Institut für Wirtschaftsforschung.

Drechsler, D., & Jütting, J. (2005b). *Private Health Insurance for the Poor in Developing Countries*, OECD Development Centre Policy Insights, (11), 7.

Drechsler, D., & Jütting, J. (2007). Different countries, different needs: The role of private health insurance in developing countries. *Journal of Health Politics, Policy and Law*, **32**(3), 497–534.

Dreze, J., & Sen, A. (2013). *An Uncertain Glory, India and Its Contradictions*. Princeton: Princeton University Press.

Drummond, M. F., Augustovski, F., Bhattacharyya, D. et al. (2022). Challenges of health technology assessment in pluralistic healthcare systems: An ISPOR council report. *Value Health*, **25**(8), 1257–67.

Economic Times. (2021). Niva Bupa Health Insurance projects Rs 5,000-cr gross written premium by 2023-24. 22 November. https://economictimes .indiatimes.com/industry/banking/finance/insure/niva-bupa-health-insur ance-projects-rs-5000-cr-gross-written-premium-by-2023-24/articleshow/ 87848435.cms?from=mdr

Ellison, J. (2014). First-class health: Amenity wards, health insurance, and normalizing health care inequalities in Tanzania. *Medical Anthropology Quarterly*, **28**(2), 162–81.

Erdoğan, C. (2020). *Expanding Supplementary Voluntary Private Health Insurance in Turkey: How and Why?*. How 'Social' Is Turkey Working Paper No.5, University of Bielefeld.

Ericson, R. V., & Doyle, A. (2006). The institutionalization of deceptive sales in life insurance: Five sources of moral risk. *British Journal of Criminology*, **46**(6), 993–1010.

Ericson, R., Barry, D., & Doyle, A. (2000a). The moral hazards of neo-liberalism: Lessons from the private insurance industry. *Economy and Society*, **29**(4), 532–58.

Ericson, R., Doyle, A., & Dean, B. (2000b). *Insurance as Governance*. Toronto: University of Toronto Press.

ET Bureau. (2021). Post-Covid increase in insurance awareness to benefit Star Health. *The Economic Times*, 25 November. https://economictimes.india times.com/markets/ipos/fpos/post-covid-increase-in-insurance-awareness-to-benefit-star-health/articleshow/87900215.cms.

Ettelt, S., & Roman-Urrestarazu, A. (2020). Statutory and private health insurance in Germany and Chile: Two stories of coexistence and conflict. In S. Thomson, A. Sagan, & E. Mossialos, eds., *Private Health Insurance History, Politics and Performance*. Cambridge: Cambridge University Press, pp. 180–220.

Financial Review. (2019). *Bupa Australia to Pay $157m to ATO*. 8 March. www.ft.com/content/8864c808-4d65-11e8-97e4-13afc22d86d4.

Fortune Business Insights. (2022). Global health insurance market size [2022–2028] to reach USD 3,038.6 billion in 2028 at a CAGR of 5.5%. *Yahoo! Finance*. https://finance.yahoo.com/news/global-health-insurance-market-size-093400250.html.

Garcia-Ramirez, J., & Nikoloski, Z. (2021). Inequality in healthcare use among older people in Colombia. *International Journal for Equity in Health*, **19**(1), 1–38.

Garg, S. (2021). Why do small businesses need group health insurance? *Economic Times*, 11 December. https://economictimes.indiatimes.com/ small-biz/money/why-do-small-businesses-need-group-health-insurance/ articleshow/88219584.cms.

Gideon, J., & Alvarez Minte, G. (2016). Institutional constraints to engendering the health sector in Bachelet's Chile. In G. Waylen, ed., *Gender, Institutions and Change in Bachelet's Chile*. New York: Palgrave Macmillan, pp. 147–60.

Goicochea, H. (2022). ILC sets sights on bond market. *LatinFinance*, January. www.latinfinance.com/daily-briefs/2022/1/26/ilc-sets-sights-on-bond-market.

Gore, A. (2015). How discovery keeps innovating commentary. *McKinsey Quarterly*, 15 May. www.mckinsey.com/industries/healthcare-systems-and-services/our-insights/how-discovery-keeps-innovating.

Greca, D., & Fitzgerald, E. (2019). *Healthcare in Brazil – Meeting Future Challenges*. https://home.kpmg/xx/en/home/insights/2019/04/meeting-healthcare-challenges-in-brazil.html.

Gupta S. (2017). Aditya Birla Health Insurance targeting young Indians through its digital strategy. *Live Mint*, 22 October. www.adityabirlacapital.com/healthinsurance/assets/pdf/supported-device-list.pdf.

Haggerty, K., Doyle, A., & Ericson, R. (2004). The police-insurance connection. *Criminal Justice Matters*, **5**(1), 28–29.

Henderson, S., & Petersen, A. (2002). *Consuming Health: The Commodification of Healthcare*. London: Routledge.

Horowitz, M. D., Rosensweig, J. A., & Jones, C. A. (2007). Medical tourism: Globalization of the healthcare marketplace. *Medscape General Medicine*, **9**(4), 1–10.

Hu, T., & Ying, X. (2010). China. In A. S. Preker, P. Zweifel, & O. P. Schellekens, eds., *Global Marketplace for Private Health Insurance – Strength in Numbers*. Washington, D C: World Bank, pp. 263–92.

Hunter, B., & Murray, S. F. (2019). Deconstructing the financialization of healthcare. *World Development*, **50**(5), 1263–87.

Hunter, B. M., Murray, S. F., Marathe, S., & Chakravarthi, I. (2022). Decentred regulation: The case of private healthcare in India. *World Development*, **155** (105889), 1–13.

ILC. (2022). *ILC en resumen*. Santiago: Inversiones La Construcción. www.ilcinversiones.cl/Spanish/quienes-somos/que-es-ilc/default.aspx.

Insurance Regulatory and Development Authority of India. (2020). *Annual Report 2020–21*, Hyderabad: IRDA.

International Trade Administration. (no date). *Chile Country Commercial Guide*. Washington, DC: U.S. Department of Commerce. www.trade.gov/chile-country-commercial-guide.

Jacobs, S. (2017). Big data comes to Africa. *This Is Africa Online*, 3 March. www.thisisafricaonline.com/.

Jain, N. (2010). *56 Million Steps towards Universal Coverage: RSBY Health Insurance for the Poor in India*. Eschborn: GTZ, 1–12.

Jeanningros, H., & McFall, L. (2020). The value of sharing: Branding and behaviour in a life and health insurance company. *Big Data & Society*, **7**(2), 1–15.

Johnston, R., Crooks, V. A., Snyder, J., & Kingsbury, P. (2010). What is known about the effects of medical tourism in destination and departure countries? A scoping review. *International Journal for Equity in Health*, **9**, 1–13.

Jost, T. (2005). Consumer-driven health care in South Africa: Lessons from comparative health policy studies. *Journal of Health and Biomedical Law*, **1**(2), 83–109.

Karwowski, E. (2019). Towards (de-)financialisation: The role of the state. *Cambridge Journal of Economics*, **43**(4), 1001–27.

Kaul, V. (2013). Hari Narayan ran Irda like an insurance lobby. *Firstpost*, 26 February. www.firstpost.com/investing/hari-narayan-ran-irda-like-an-insurance-lobby-640487.html.

Kochhar, R. (2021). The pandemic stalls growth in the global middle class, pushes poverty up sharply. *Pew Research Center Report*, 18 March, Washington, DC. www.pewresearch.org/global/2021/03/18/.

Koivusalo, M., & Sexton, S. (2016). Gender and commercialization of health care. In J. Gideon, ed., *Handbook on Gender and Health*. Cheltenham: Edward Elgar, pp. 298–308.

Koivusalo, M., Heinonen, N., & Tynkkynen, L. K. (2021). When actions do not match aspirations – comparison of the European Union policy claims against what has been negotiated for health services, trade and investment. *Globalization and Health*, **17**(198), 1–11

Krishna, A. (2011). *One Illness Away: Why People Become Poor and How They Escape Poverty*. Oxford: Oxford University Press.

Kulkarni, P. (2020). Are hospitals overcharging for COVID treatment? Insurers to analyse claims data. *Moneycontrol*, 6 May, Mumbai: Network 18 group. www.moneycontrol.com/europe/?url=https://www.moneycontrol.com/news/business/personal-finance/are-hospitals-overcharging-for-covid-treatment-insurers-to-analyse-claims-data-5228341.html.

Kulkarni, P. (2021). Mis-selling and claim rejections top complaints at insurance ombudsman. *Moneycontrol*, 18 November, Mumbai: Network 18 group. www.moneycontrol.com/europe/?url=https://www.moneycontrol.com/news/business/personal-finance/mis-selling-and-claim-rejections-top-complaints-at-insurance-ombudsman-7729671.html.

Kulkarni, S. (2022). Does your health insurance company have the money to pay your claim? Check here. *The Economic Times*, 11 January. https://

economictimes.indiatimes.com/wealth/insure/health-insurance/does-your-health-insurance-company-have-the-money-to-pay-your-claim-check-here/articleshow/88830845.cms.

Kutzin, J., Yip, W., & Cashin, C. (2016). Alternative financing strategies for universal health coverage. In R. M. Scheffler, ed., *World Scientific Handbook of Global Health Economics and Public Policy*. Singapore: World Scientific, pp. 267–309.

Lamprea, E., & García, J. (2016). Closing the gap between formal and material health care coverage in Colombia. *Health and Human Rights*, **18**(2), 49–65.

Laskar, A. (2022). Will the third wave push up health insurance premiums? *Mint E-Paper*, 12 January. www.livemint.com/insurance/news/insurers-weigh-hike-in-health-premiums-11641926109610.html.

Lavinas, L. (2017). *The Takeover of Social Policy by Financialization: The Brazilian Paradox*. London: Palgrave Macmillan. https://doi.org/10.1057/978-1-137-49107-7.

Lee, K. (2009). *The World Health Organization (WHO)*. Oxford: Routledge.

Lehtonen, T. K., & Liukko, J. (2010). Justifications for commodified security: The promotion of private life insurance in Finland 1945–90. *Acta Sociologica*, **53**(4), 371–86.

Lehtonen, T. K., & Liukko, J. (2011). The forms and limits of insurance solidarity. *Journal of Business Ethics*, **103**(Suppl1), 33–44.

Lehtonen, T. K., & Liukko, J. (2015). Producing solidarity, inequality and exclusion through insurance. *Res Publica*, **21**(2), 155–69.

Lehtonen, T. K., & Van Hoyweghen, I. (2014). Editorial: Insurance and the economization of uncertainty. *Journal of Cultural Economy*, **7**(4), 532–40.

Lei, D. (2015). China focus: Tax rebate policy to spur growth in China's private health insurance. *Xinhua Economic News Service*, 7 May, Beijing: Xinhua News Agency.

Lendner, P. (2018). Medical tourism: Once ready for takeoff, now stuck at the gate. *Managed Care*, **27**(4), 30–41.

Leng, C. (2022). Huiminbao added about 100 million new customers last year, experts put forward four suggestions. *Teller Report*: China News, 10 February. www.tellerreport.com/business/2022–02-10-huiminbao-added-about-100-million-new-customers-last-year-experts-put-forward-four-suggestions.HJVEnexmJ5.html.

Lethbridge, J. (2005a). Strategies of multinational health care companies in Europe and Asia. In M. Mackintosh & & M. Koivusalo, eds., *Commercialization of Health Care: Global and Local Dynamics and Policy Responses*. London: Palgrave Macmillan, pp. 22–37.

Lethbridge, J. (2005b). The promotion of investment alliances by the World Bank: Implications for national health policy. *Global Social Policy*, **5**(2), 203–25.

Lethbridge, J. (2011). Understanding multinational companies in public health systems, using a competitive advantage framework. *Globalization and Health*, **7**, 1–10.

Lethbridge, J. (2015). *Health Care Reforms and the Rise of Global Multinational Health Care Companies*. A briefing paper commissioned by Public Services International (PSI). London. www.world-psi.org.

Lethbridge, J. (2017). World Bank undermines right to universal healthcare. London: Bretton Woods Project Briefing, 1–4.

Leverty, J. T., Lin, Y., & Zhou, H. (2009). WTO and the Chinese insurance industry. *Geneva Papers on Risk and Insurance: Issues and Practice*, **34**(3), 440–65.

Light, D. W. (2003). Universal health care: Lessons from the British experience. *American Journal of Public Health*, **93**(1), 25–30.

Live Mint. (2013). Regulators are sometimes too close to industry: Hari Narayan. *Im4change*, 21 February. www.im4change.org/latest-news-updates/regulators-are-sometimes-too-close-to-industry-hari-narayan-deepti-bhaskaran-19547.html.

Live Mint. (2021). Plum launches Lite, a health benefit membership for gig workers. *Livemint.Com*, 21 December. www.livemint.com/companies/news/plum-launches-lite-a-health-benefit-membership-for-gig-workers-11640075 623127.html.

Live Mint. (2022). Mahindra Lifespaces offers group health insurance for homebuyers. *Livemint.Com*, 9 February. www.livemint.com/companies/news/mahindra-lifespaces-offers-group-health-insurance-for-homebuyers-11644380712982.html.

Lunt, N., Smith, R., Exworthy, et al. (2011). *Medical Tourism: Treatments, Markets and Health System Implications: A Scoping Review*. Paris: OECD Directorate for Employment, Labour and Social Affairs, 1–55.

Machado, C. V., & Silva, G. A. E. (2019). Political struggles for a universal health system in Brazil: Successes and limits in the reduction of inequalities. *Globalization and Health*, **15**(Suppl 1), 17, 1–12. https://doi.org/10.1186/s12992-019-0523-5.

Mackintosh, M., & Koivusalo, M. (2005). Health systems and commercialization: In search of good sense. In M. Mackintosh, & M. Koivusalo, eds., *Commercialization of Health Care: Global and Local Dynamics and Policy Responses*. London: Palgrave Macmillan, pp. 3–21.

Mahindra Lifespaces. (2022). Mahindra Lifespaces is crafting life at India's first health sampanna homes. *The Times of India*, 30 March, Mumbai.

Maiti, M. (2021). Omicron scare: What kind of health insurance should you buy for your parents? *Outlook*, 13 December. www.outlookindia.com/website/story/business-news-omicron-scare-what-kind-of-health-insurance-should-you-buy-for-your-parents/404639.

Marriage, M. (2018). Bupa under investigation by Australian tax authorities. *Financial Times*, 2 May. www.ft.com/content/8864c808-4d65-11e8-97e4-13afc22d86d4.

Marshall, E. (2022). Brazilian health insurance premiums face biggest hike in 22 years. *The Brazilian Report*, 26 May. https://brazilian.report/liveblog/2022/05/26/health-insurance-premiums-hike.

Mathauer, I., & Kutzin, J. (2018). *Voluntary Health Insurance: Potentials and Limits in Moving towards UCH*, Health Financing Policy Brief No. 5, Geneva: World Health Organization, 1–10.

Mathauer, I., Saksena, P., & Kutzin, J. (2019). Pooling arrangements in health financing systems: A proposed classification. *International Journal for Equity in Health*, **18**(1), 1–11.

Mawdsley, E., Murray, W. E., Overton, J., Scheyvens, R., & Banks, G. (2018). Exporting stimulus and 'shared prosperity': Reinventing foreign aid for a retroliberal era. *Development Policy Review*, **36**, O25–43.

McFall, L., Meyers, G., & Van Hoyweghen, I. (2020). Editorial: The personalisation of insurance: Data, behaviour and innovation. *Big Data & Society*. July–December, 1–11.

McIntyre, D., & McLeod, H. (2020). The challenges of pursuing private health insurance in low- and middle income countries: Lessons from South Africa. In S. Thomson, A. Sagan, & E. Mossialos, eds., *Private Health Insurance History, Politics and Performance*. Cambridge: Cambridge University Press, pp. 377–413.

McKee, M., & Stuckler, D. (2018). Revisiting the corporate and commercial determinants of health. *American Journal of Public Health*, **108**(9), 1167–70.

McLeod, H., & McIntyre, D. (2020). Undermining risk pooling by individualizing benefits: The use of medical savings accounts in South Africa. In S. Thomson, A. Sagan, & E. Mossialos, eds., *Private Health Insurance History, Politics and Performance*. Cambridge: Cambridge University Press, pp. 414–55.

Mialon, M. (2020). An overview of the commercial determinants of health. *Globalization and Health*, **16**(1), 1–7.

Ministerio de Salud y Protección Social. (2022). Colombia reached universal health insurance at 99.6%. Press Release No. 373, 29 June. www.minsalud

.gov.co/English/Paginas/Colombia-Reached-Universal-Health-Insurance-at-99.aspx.

Miraftab, F. (2004). Public-private partnerships: The Trojan horse of neoliberal development? *Journal of Planning Education and Research*, **24**(1), 89–101.

Mohan, A. V., McCormick, D., Woolhandler, S., Himmelstein, D. U., & Boyd, J. W. (2010). Life and health insurance industry investments in fast food. *American Journal of Public Health*, **100**(6), 1029–30.

Montoya Diaz, M. D., Haber, N., Mladovsky, P. et al. (2020). Private health insurance in Brazil, Egypt and India. In S. Thomson, A. Sagan, & E. Mossialos, eds., *Private Health Insurance History, Politics and Performance*. Cambridge: Cambridge University Press, pp. 65–98.

Mulligan, J. (2016). Insurance accounts: The cultural logics of health care financing. *Medical Anthropology Quarterly*, **30**(1), 37–61.

Murray, S. F. (2016). Commercialization in maternity care: Uncovering trends in the contemporary health care economy. In J. Gideon, ed., *Handbook on Gender and Health*. Cheltenham: Edward Elgar, pp. 309–26.

Murray, S. F., & Elston, M. A. (2005). The promotion of private health insurance and its implications for the social organisation of healthcare: A case study of private sector obstetric practice in Chile. *Sociology of Health and Illness*, **27**(6), 701–21.

Ng, A., Süssmuth-Dyckerhoff, C., & Then, F. (2012). Private health insurance in China: Finding the winning formula. *Health International*, **12**, 75–82. McKinsey.

NHS Shared Business Services. (2018). Insourcing of clinical services framework agreement description. Reference: SBS/18/CW/ZOC/9314. Hemel Hempstead: NHS Shared Business Services. www.sbs.nhs.uk/article/17314/Insourcing-of-Clinical-Services.

Ocké-Reis, C. O. (1995). *O setor privado de saúde no Brasil: os limites da autonomia*. Rio de Janeiro: IMS/UERJ.

OECD/European Union. (2018). Health at a Glance: Europe 2018: State of Health in the EU Cycle, OECD Publishing, Paris. https://doi.org/10.1787/health_glance_eur-2018-en .

Okorafor, O. A. (2012). National health insurance reform in South Africa. *Applied Health Economics and Health Policy*, **10**(3), 189–200.

Ollila, E., & Koivusalo, M. (2002). The World Health Report 2000: World Health Organization health policy steering off course – changed values, poor evidence, and lack of accountability. *International Journal of Health Services*, **32**(3), 503–14.

Organisation for Economic Co-operation and Development. (2022a). *OECDStat*. https://stats.oecd.org/index.aspx?queryid=30139.

Organisation for Economic Co-operation and Development. (2022b). *OECD Health Statistics 2022 Definitions, Sources and Methods: Voluntary Health Insurance.* www.oecd.org/health/health-data.htm.

Ormond, M. (2013). *Neoliberal Governance and International Medical Travel in Malaysia.* Abingdon: Routledge.

Ossandón, J. (2014). Reassembling and cutting the social with health insurance. *Journal of Cultural Economy*, **7**(3), 291–307.

Ossandón, J. (2015). The enactment of economic things: The objects of insurance. In M. Kornberger, L. Justesen, A. K. Madsen, & J. Mouritsen, eds., *Making Things Valuable.* Oxford: Oxford University Press, pp. 583–605.

Ossandón, J., & Ureta, S. (2019). Problematizing markets: Market failures and the government of collective concerns. *Economy and Society*, **48**(2), 175–96.

Pollock, A., & Roderick, P. (2021). If you believe in a public NHS, the new health and care bill should set off alarm bells. Opinion NHS. *The Guardian*, 7 December. www.theguardian.com/commentisfree/2021/dec/07/public-nhs-the-new-health-and-care-bill-alarm-bells-privatisation.

Prainsack, B. (2020). The value of healthcare data_ to nudge, or not? *Policy Studies*, **41**(5), 547–62.

Prainsack, B., & Buyx, A. (2014). Nudging and solidarity: Do they go together? *Eurohealth*, **20**(2), 14–17.

Prainsack, B., & Buyx, A. (2017). *Solidarity in Biomedicine and beyond.* Cambridge: Cambridge University Press.

Preker, A. S., Cotlear, D., Kwon, S., Atun, R., & Avila, C. (2021). Universal health care in middle-income countries: Lessons from four countries. *Journal of Global Health*, **20**(11), 1–17.

Preker, A. S., Scheffler, R. M., & Bassett, M. C. (2007). *Private Voluntary Health Insurance in Development: Friend or Foe?* Washington, DC: The World Bank.

Preker, A. S., Zweifel, P., & Schellekens, O. P., eds., (2010). *Global Marketplace for Private Health Insurance: Strength in Numbers.* Washington, DC: The World Bank.

Press Trust of India. (2021). Equitas SFB, Cholamandalam MS for women-centric health insurance policy. *Business Standard News*, 13 December. www.business-standard.com/article/finance/equitas-sfb-cholamandalam-ms-for-women-centric-health-insurance-policy-121121300646_1.html.

Prince, R. (2017). Universal health coverage in the global South: New models of healthcare and their implications for citizenship, solidarity, and the public good. *Michael*, **14**, 153–72.

PwC. (2013). *The Healthcare Market in Brazil.* 1–12. www.pwc.com.br/pt/publicacoes/setores-atividade/assets/saude/healthcare-tsp-13.pdf.

Rao, U. (2010). Neoliberalism and the rewriting of the Indian leader. *American Ethnologist*, **37**(4), 713–25.

Reeves, R. V, Guyot, K., & Monday, E. K. (2018). *Defining the middle class: Cash, credentials, or culture?* Middle Class Memos. Washington, DC: Brookings Institution.

ResearchAndMarkets.com. (2022). Global insurance analytics market (2022 to 2027) – industry trends, share, size, growth, opportunity and forecasts. *Businesswire*, 22 March, Dublin. www.businesswire.com/news/home/20220322005669/en.

Robyn, P. J., Sauerborn, R., & Bärnighausen, T. (2013). Provider payment in community-based health insurance schemes in developing countries: A systematic review. *Health Policy and Planning*, **28**(2), 111–22.

Rose, N. (1999). *Powers of Freedom Reframing Political Thought*. Cambridge: Cambridge University Press. https://doi.org/10.1017/CBO9780511488856.

Ruiz. A. (2019). *Lavín y Délano comenzaron las clases de ética tras condena del caso Penta*. Santiago: 24Horas.cl TVN, 5 April. www.24horas.cl/politica/lavin-y-delano-comenzaron-las-clases-de-etica-tras-condena-del-caso-penta-3218640.

Sandel, M. J. (2012). *What Money Can't Buy: The Moral Limits of Markets*. New York: Farrar, Straus and Giroux.

Sarkar, B. (2021). GigVistas partners with Alyve Health to launch health plans for gig workers. *The Economic Times*, 23 December. https://economictimes.indiatimes.com/industry/banking/finance/insure/gigvistas-partners-with-alyve-health-to-launch-health-plans-for-gig-workers/articleshow/88450862.cms?from=mdr.

Sarwal, R., & Kumar, A. (2021). *Health Insurance for India's Missing Middle*. Delhi: NITI Aayog. www.niti.gov.in/sites/default/files/2021-10/HealthInsurance-forIndiasMissingMiddle_28-10-2021.pdf.

Satz, D. (2010). *Why Some Things Should Not Be for Sale: The Moral Limits of Markets*. Oxford: Oxford University Press. https://doi.org/10.1093/acprof:oso/9780195311594.001.0001.

Scheffer, M., & Bahia, L. (2013). O financiamento de campanhas pelos planos e seguros de saúde nas eleições de 2010. *Saúde Em Debate*, **37**(96), 96–103.

Scheffer, M. C., Pastor-Valero, M., Russo, G., & Hernández-Aguado, I. (2020). Revolving doors and conflicts of interest in health regulatory agencies in Brazil. *BMJ Global Health*, **5**(4), 3–7.

Science Media Centre. (2021). Expert reaction to press release from discovery health giving real-world information on their Omicron outbreak based on 211000 COVID-19 positive test results in South Africa. 14 December.

www.sciencemediacentre.org/expert-reaction-to-press-release-from-discovery-health-giving-real-world-information-on-their-omicron-outbreak-based-on-211000-covid-19-positive-test-results-in-south-africa/.

Sekhri, N., & Savedoff, W. (2005). Private health insurance: Implications for developing countries. *Bulletin of the World Health Organization*, **83**(2), 127–34.

Sekhri, N., & Savedoff, W. (2006). Regulating private health insurance to serve the public interest: Policy issues for developing countries. *International Journal of Health Planning and Management*, **21**(4), 357–92.

Shanghai Municipal People's Government. (2020). Supplemental health insurance spreads among population. 2 December. https://english.shanghai.gov .cn/nw48088/20201202/453504e784c34458acb18530a4a6a04c.html.

Shangquan, G. (2000). *Economic Globalization: Trends, Risks and Risk Prevention*, Vol. 1. New York. www.un.org/en/development/desa/policy/ cdp/cdp_background_papers/bp2000_1.pdf.

Shi, J., & Liu G. (2018). Health insurance and payment system reform in China. In T. G. McGuire, & R. C. van Kleef, eds., *Risk Adjustment, Risk Sharing and Premium Regulation in Health Insurance Markets: Theory and Practice*. Amsterdam: Elsevier, pp. 263–78.

Silvello, A., & Procaccini, A. (2019). Connected insurance reshaping the health insurance industry, In T. F .Heston, ed., *Smart Healthcare*. London: IntechOpen, pp. 1–15.

Sinha, S. (2021). What does a super top-up health insurance policy cost? Compare premiums. *Financial Express*, 24 December. www.financialex press.com/money/insurance/what-does-a-super-top-up-health-insurance-policy-cost-compare-premiums/2388659/.

Sinha, S., & Rajagopal, D. (2017). Max Bupa, hospital lobby group sparover generic drug prescription. *The Economic Times*, 12 May, Mumbai. https:// economictimes.indiatimes.com/articleshow/58634898.cms?from=mdr.

Sio, R. (2019). China to let insurers invest in tier 2 bond. *S&P Global*, 24 January. www.spglobal.com/marketintelligence/en/news-insights/trend ing/or4_dX2dG7d1vciEInRZOQ2.

Slater, D., & Tonkiss, F. (2000). *Market Society: Markets and Modern Social Theory*. Malden: Polity Press.

Soderlund, N., & Hansl, B. (2000). Health insurance in South Africa: An empirical analysis of trends in risk-pooling and efficiency following deregulation. *Health Policy and Planning*, **15**(4), 378–85.

Soloman, A. (2014). Purging the legacy of dictatorship from Chile's constitution. *The Nation*, 21 January. www.thenation.com/article/archive/purging-legacy-dictatorship-chiles-constitution/.

Sparkes, S. P., Kutzin, J., & Earle, A. J. (2019). Financing common goods for health: A country agenda. *Health Systems and Reform*, **5**(4), 322–33.

Spender, A., Bullen, C., Altmann-Richer, L. et al. (2019). Wearables and the internet of things: Considerations for the life and health insurance industry. *British Actuarial Journal*, **24**, 1–31.

Srinivas, A. (2020). The covid-19 boost to health insurance, in four charts. *Mint E-Paper*. www.livemint.com/insurance/news/the-covid-19-boost-to-health-insurance-in-four-charts-11605597369780.html.

Stein, F., & Sridhar, D. (2018). The financialisation of global health. *Wellcome Open Research*, **3**(17), 1–4.

Stenberg, K., Hanssen, O., Edejer, T., & Soucat, A. (2017). Financing transformative health systems towards achievement of the health sustainable development goals: A model for projected resource needs in 67 low-income and middle-income countries. *The Lancet Global Health*, **5**(9), e875–87.

Sun, Q. (2005). The interactions between social and commercial health insurance after China's entry into the World Trade Organization. In M. Mackintosh, & M. Koivusalo, eds., *Commercialization of Health Care: Global and Local Dynamics and Policy Responses*. London: Palgrave Macmillan, pp. 84–100.

Tessier, L., Behrendt, C., & Markov, K. (2020). *Towards Universal Health Coverage: Social Health Protection Principles*. Social Protection Spotlight. International Labour Organization Brief. Geneva: ILO.

Thomas, T. K. (2016). Role of health insurance in enabling universal health coverage in India: A critical review. *Health Services Management Research*, **29**(4), 99–106.

Thomson, S., Sagan, A., & Mossialos, E. (2020a). *Private Health Insurance: History, Politics and Performance*. Cambridge: European Observatory on Health Systems and Policies and Cambridge University Press.

Thomson, S., Sagan, A., & Mossialos, E. (2020b). Why private health insurance? In S. Thomson, A. Sagan, & E. Mossialos, eds., *Private Health Insurance History, Politics and Performance*. Cambridge: Cambridge University Press, pp. 1–40.

Tritter, J., Koivusalo, M., Ollila, E., & Dorfman, P. (2009). *Globalisation, Markets and Healthcare Policy: Redrawing the Patient as Consumer*. London: Taylor & Francis Group. https://doi.org/10.4324/9780203875094.

Triunfol, M. (2022). High hopes for a healthier Brazil with Lula's third mandate. *The Lancet Oncology*, **23**(12), e533.

Vargas Bustamante, A., & Méndez, C. A. (2014). Health care privatization in Latin America: Comparing divergent privatization approaches in Chile,

Colombia, and Mexico. *Journal of Health Politics, Policy and Law*, **39**(4), 841–86.

Vargas Bustamante, A., & Méndez, C. A. (2016). Regulating self-selection into private health insurance in Chile and the United States. *The International Journal of Health Planning and Management*, **31**(3), e219–34.

Vargas, I., Vazquez, M. L., Mogollán-Pérez, A. S., & Unger, J. P. (2010). Barriers of access to care in a managed competition model: Lessons from Colombia. *BMC Health Services Research*, **10**(297), 1–12. https://doi.org/10.1186/1472-6963-10-297.

Vitality. (2021). Neville Koopowitz: What we really mean by 'shared value' health insurance. *Cover Magazine*, 19 November. www.covermagazine.co.uk/sponsored/4040667/neville-koopowitz-mean-shared-value-health-insurance.

Vitality Health International Press Release. (2022). Vitality Health International introduces vitality rewards across Africa. *Discovery Holdings Ltd*, 2 February. www.mynewsdesk.com/za/discovery-holdings-ltd/pressreleases/vitality-health-international-introduces-vitality-rewards-across-africa-3159076.

Wagstaff, A., & Neelsen, S. (2020). A comprehensive assessment of universal health coverage in 111 countries: A retrospective observational study. *The Lancet Global Health*, **8**(1), e39–49.

Wang, H. (2009). The developments and future prospects of insurance industry in China. *International Journal of Business and Management*, **4**(6), 150–3.

Weber, I. (2020). Origins of China's contested relation with neoliberalism: Economics, the World Bank, and Milton Friedman at the dawn of reform. *Global Perspectives*, **1**(1), 1–14.

Wildau, G. (2019). Wealthy Chinese spur booming $78bn health insurance industry. *Financial Times*, 8 January. www.ft.com/content/2e3e9af6-fd10-11e8-aebf-99e208d3e521.

Wilmot, J. (2017). *DA Demands Regulatory Impact Assessment of Ban on Private Health Insurance for the Poor*. Media Statement, 10 January. www.polity.org.za/article/da-wilmot-james-says-da-demands-regulatory-impact-assessment-of-ban-on-private-health-insurance-for-the-poor-2017-01-10.

World Bank. (1993). *World Development Report 1993: Investing in Health. Economic Development and Cultural Change*, Vol. 45. Washington, DC: World Bank. https://doi.org/10.1596/978-0-19-520890-0.

World Bank. (1997). *Health, Nutrition and Population Sector Strategy*. Washington, DC: World Bank. https://elibrary.worldbank.org/doi/abs/10.1596/0-8213-4040-9.

World Bank. (2004). *Rural Health in China: Taking Stock of China's Rural Health Challenges.* Briefing Notes Series Note No. 1. 33231, October, 1–8. Washington, DC: World Bank. https://documents1.worldbank.org/curated/en/798831468214496104/text/332310ENGLISH0CHA0BN1.txt.

World Bank. (2018). *Healthy China: Deepening Health Reform by Building High-Quality and Value-Based Service Delivery.* 16 April, Results Brief. Washington, DC: World Bank, IBRD, IDA. www.worldbank.org/en/results/2018/04/16/healthy-china-deepening-health-reform-by-building-high-quality-value-based-service-delivery.

World Bank. (2019). *Health Financing for High-Performance Coverage for Universal Health Coverage: Driving Sustainable, Inclusive Growth in the 21st Century.* Washington, DC: World Bank. http://documents.worldbank.org/curated/en/641451561043585615/Driving-Sustainable-Inclusive-Growth-in-the-21st-Century.

World Bank. (2020). *A Comprehensive Assessment of Universal Health Coverage in 111 Countries: A Retrospective Observational Study.* Washington, DC: World Bank. https://datacatalog.worldbank.org/search/dataset/0038533.

World Bank. (2022a). *New World Bank Country Classifications by Income level 2022–2023.* 1 July. https://blogs.worldbank.org/opendata/new-world-bank-country-classifications-income-level-2022-2023.

World Bank. (2022b). Middle income countries program: Overview. 29 August. www.worldbank.org/en/country/mic/overview.

World Bank and International Monetary Fund. (2015). *From Billions to Trillions: Transforming Development Finance.* Washington, DC: World Bank.

World Bank, & World Trade Organization. (2022). *Trade Therapy: Deepening Cooperation to Strengthen Pandemic Defenses.* Washington, DC: World Bank Group.

World Health Organization. (2000). World health report: Health systems: Improving performance. Geneva: WHO

World Population Review. (2023). Country estimates. https://worldpopulationreview.com.

Wu, R., Li, N., & Ercia, A. (2020). The effects of private health insurance on universal health coverage objectives in China: A systematic literature review. *International Journal of Environmental Research and Public Health*, **17**(6), 1–21.

Xinhua News Agency. (2007). *China Encourages Insurers to Invest Abroad.* www.china.org.cn/business/news/2007-11/30/content_1234006.htm.

Yadavalli, S. P. (2022). Why health insurance is a must for some. *The Hindu Business Line*, 12 February. www.thehindubusinessline.com/.

Yi, R., & Huang, S. (2019). China's commercial health insurance market. *Asia Insurance Review*, March. www.asiainsurancereview.com/Magazine/ReadMagazineArticle/aid/41884/SharedCode/0A5C27/China-s-commercial-health-insurance-market/1.

Yilmaz, V. (2013). Changing origins of inequalities in access to health care services in Turkey: From occupational status to income. *New Perspectives on Turkey*, **48**(48), 55–77.

Zhang, S., & Yang, M. (2007). The world trade organization and China's health insurance sector. In M. Wang, S. Zhang, & X. Wang, eds., *WTO, Globalization and China's Health Care System*. London: Palgrave Macmillan, pp. 40–54.

Acknowledgements

Many thanks are due to the Development Studies series editors, the anonymous reviewers, and to my colleague Dr Ben Hunter for the incisive critique and suggestions during the development of this manuscript.

My thanks to Dr Sofía González De Aguinaga for her assistance with an early search for relevant literature.

Cambridge Elements ⹂

Global Development Studies

Peter Ho
Zhejiang University

Peter Ho is Distinguished Professor at Zhejiang University and high-level National Expert of China. He has held or holds the position of, amongst others, Research Professor at the London School of Economics and Political Science and the School of Oriental and African Studies, Full Professor at Leiden University and Director of the Modern East Asia Research Centre, Full Professor at Groningen University and Director of the Centre for Development Studies. Ho is well-cited and published in leading journals of development, planning and area studies. He published numerous books, including with *Cambridge University Press*, *Oxford University Press*, and *Wiley-Blackwell*. Ho achieved the William Kapp Prize, China Rural Development Award, and European Research Council Consolidator Grant. He chairs the International Conference on Agriculture and Rural Development (www.icardc.org) and sits on the boards of *Land Use Policy*, *Conservation and Society*, *China Rural Economics*, *Journal of Peasant Studies*, and other journals.

Servaas Storm
Delft University of Technology

Servaas Storm is a Dutch economist who has published widely on issues of macroeconomics, development, income distribution & economic growth, finance, and climate change. He is a Senior Lecturer at Delft University of Technology. He obtained a PhD in Economics (in 1992) from Erasmus University Rotterdam and worked as consultant for the ILO and UNCTAD. His latest book, co-authored with C.W.M. Naastepad, is *Macroeconomics Beyond the NAIRU* (Harvard University Press, 2012) and was awarded with the 2013 Myrdal Prize of the European Association for Evolutionary Political Economy. Servaas Storm is one of the editors of *Development and Change* (2006-now) and a member of the Institute for New Economic Thinking's Working Group on the Political Economy of Distribution.

About the Series

The Cambridge Elements on Global Development Studies publishes ground-breaking, novel works that move beyond existing theories and methodologies of development in order to consider social change in real times and real spaces.

Cambridge Elements ≡

Global Development Studies

Elements in the Series

Temporary Migrants from Southeast Asia in Australia: Lost Opportunities
Juliet Pietsch

Mobile (for) Development: When Digital Giants Take Care of Poor Women
Marine Al Dahdah

Displacement in War-torn Ukraine: State, Dislocation and Belonging
Viktoriya Sereda

Investor States: Global Health at the End of Aid
Benjamin M. Hunter

Global Health Worker Migration: Problems and Solutions
Margaret Walton-Roberts

Going Public: The Unmaking and Remaking of Universal Healthcare
Ramya Kumar and Anne-Emanuelle Birn

The Problem of Private Health Insurance: Insights from Middle-Income Countries
Susan F Murray

A full series listing is available at: www.cambridge.org/EGDS

Printed in the United States
by Baker & Taylor Publisher Services